KINGDOM MEN RISING

TONY EVANS

Lifeway Press®
Nashville, Tennessee

EDITORIAL TEAM

Heather Hair
Writer

Reid Patton
Content Editor

Susan Hill
Production Editor

Jon Rodda
Art Director

Joel Polk
Editorial Team Leader

Brian Daniel
Manager, Adult Discipleship

Brandon Hiltibidal
Director, Discipleship and Adult Ministry

Published by Lifeway Press® · © 2021 Tony Evans ·

ISBN 978-1-0877-2973-2 · Item 005829344

DEWEY: 248.842

Subhead: MEN / HUSBANDS / FATHERS

My deepest thanks go to Mrs. Heather Hair for her skills and insights in collaboration on this manuscript.
Scripture quotations are taken from the New American Standard Bible®, Copyright © 1960, 1962, 1963, 1968, 1971, 1972, 1973, 1975, 1977, 1995 by The Lockman Foundation. Used by permission. (www.lockman.org)

Scripture quotations marked (NIV) are taken from the Holy Bible, New International Version®, NIV®. Copyright © 1973, 1978, 1984, 2011 by Biblica, Inc.TM Used by permission of Zondervan. All rights reserved worldwide. www.zondervan.com. The "NIV" and "New International Version" are trademarks registered in the United States Patent and Trademark Office by Biblica, Inc.TM

To order additional copies of this resource, write to Lifeway Resources Customer Service; One Lifeway Plaza; Nashville, TN 37234; fax 615-251-5933; call toll free 800-458-2772; order online at Lifeway.com; or email orderentry@lifeway.com.

Printed in the United States of America

Adult Ministry Publishing · Lifeway Resources · One Lifeway Plaza · Nashville, TN 37234

CONTENTS

ABOUT THE AUTHOR

DR. TONY EVANS is one of the country's most respected leaders in evangelical circles. He is a pastor, best-selling author and frequent speaker at Bible conferences and seminars throughout the nation.

Dr. Evans has served as the senior pastor of Oak Cliff Bible Fellowship for over 40 years, witnessing its growth from ten people in 1976 to now over 10,000 congregants with over 100 ministries.

Dr. Evans also serves as president of The Urban Alternative, a national ministry that seeks to restore hope and transform lives through the proclamation and application of the Word of God. His daily radio broadcast, The Alternative with Dr. Tony Evans, can be heard on over 1,400 radio outlets throughout the United States and in more than 130 countries.

Dr. Evans holds the honor of writing and publishing the first full-Bible commentary and study Bible by an African American. The study Bible and Commentary went on to sell more than 225,000 in the first year.

Dr. Evans is the former chaplain for the Dallas Cowboys and the Dallas Mavericks.

Through his local church and national ministry, Dr. Evans has set in motion a kingdom agenda philosophy of ministry that teaches God's comprehensive rule over every area of life as demonstrated through the individual, family, church and society.

Dr. Evans was married to Lois, his wife and ministry partner of over 50 years until Lois transitioned to glory in late 2019. They are the proud parents of four, grandparents of thirteen and great-grandparents of three.

ABOUT THE URBAN ALTERNATIVE

The Urban Alternative (TUA) is a Christian broadcast and teaching ministry founded more than thirty-five years ago by Dr. Tony Evans. TUA seeks to promote a kingdom agenda philosophy designed to enable people to live all of life underneath the comprehensive rule of God. This is accomplished through a variety of means, including media, resources, clergy ministries, and community-impact training.

KINGDOM MEN RISING

TONY EVANS

HOW TO GET THE MOST FROM THIS STUDY

This Bible-study book includes eight weeks of content for group and personal study.

GROUP SESSIONS

Regardless of what day of the week your group meets, each week of content begins with the group session. Each group session uses the following format to facilitate simple yet meaningful interaction among group members, with God's Word, and with the teaching of Dr. Evans.

START. This page includes questions to get the conversation started and to introduce the video teaching.

WATCH. This page includes key points from Dr. Evans's teaching so that participants can follow along as they watch the video.

MAN UP. This page includes questions and statements that guide the group to respond to Dr. Evans's video teaching and to relevant Bible passages.

PERSONAL STUDY

Each week provides three days of Bible study and learning activities for individual engagement between group sessions: "Hit the Streets" and two Bible studies.

HIT THE STREETS. This section highlights practical steps for taking the week's teaching and putting it into practice.

BIBLE STUDIES. These personal studies revisit stories, Scriptures, and themes Dr. Evans introduced in the videos so that men can understand and apply them on a personal level. Men should use the other days of the week to reflect on what God is teaching them and to practice putting the biblical principles into action.

D-GROUP GUIDES

In addition to the group sessions and personal studies, D-Group guides are provided in the back of this Bible study book. These guides correspond to the eight weeks of study and are designed to be used in a smaller group of three or four men for deeper discussion and accountability. Each week includes a guide for smaller-group discussion. Each guide provides helpful thoughts on the week's content and suggests a few questions for discussion by and accountability among the group.

TIPS FOR LEADING A SMALL GROUP

Follow these guidelines to prepare for each group session.

PRAYERFULLY PREPARE

REVIEW. Review the weekly material and group questions ahead of time.

PRAY. Be intentional about praying for each person in the group.

Ask the Holy Spirit to work through you and the group discussion as you point to Jesus each week through God's Word.

MINIMIZE DISTRACTIONS

Create a comfortable environment. If group members are uncomfortable, they'll be distracted and therefore not engaged in the group experience. Plan ahead by considering these details, include seating, temperature, lighting, food and drink, and general cleanliness. Do everything in your ability to help people focus on what's most important: connecting with God, with the Bible, and with one another.

ENCOURAGE DISCUSSION

A good small-group experience has the following characteristics.

EVERYONE IS INCLUDED. Your goal is to foster a community in which people are welcome just as they are but encouraged to grow spiritually. Always be aware of opportunities to include any people who visit the group and to invite new people to join your group.

EVERYONE PARTICIPATES. Encourage everyone to ask questions, share responses, or read aloud.

NO ONE DOMINATES—NOT EVEN THE LEADER. Be sure that your time speaking as a leader takes up less than half of your time together as a group. Politely guide discussion if anyone dominates.

NOBODY IS RUSHED THROUGH QUESTIONS. Don't feel that a moment of silence is a bad thing. People often need time to think about their responses to questions they've just heard or to gain courage to share what God is stirring in their hearts.

INPUT IS AFFIRMED AND FOLLOWED UP. Make sure you point out something true or helpful in a response. Don't just move on. Build community with follow-up questions, asking how other people have experienced similar things or how a truth has shaped their understanding of God and the Scripture you're studying. People are less likely to speak up if they fear that you don't actually want to hear their answers or that you're looking for only a certain answer.

GOD AND HIS WORD ARE CENTRAL. Opinions and experiences can be helpful, but God has given us the truth. Trust God's Word to be the authority and God's Spirit to work in people's lives. You can't change anyone, but God can. Continually point people to the Word and to active steps of faith.

KEEP CONNECTING

Think of ways to connect with group members during the week. Participation during the group session is always improved when members spend time connecting with one another outside the group sessions. The more people are comfortable with and involved in one another's lives, the more they'll look forward to being together. When people move beyond being friendly to truly being friends who form a community, they come to each session eager to engage instead of merely attending.

Encourage group members with thoughts, commitments, or questions from the session by connecting through these communication channels:

Emails / Texts / Social Media

When possible, build deeper friendships by planning or spontaneously inviting group members to join you outside your regularly scheduled group time for activities like these:

Meals / Fun Activities
Projects around Your Home, Church, or Community

And if you belong to Christ, then
you are Abraham's descendants,
heirs according to promise.

GALATIANS 3:29

WEEK 1
CHOSEN FOR THE CHALLENGE

START

Welcome to group session 1 of *Kingdom Men Rising.*

When building a house, what is the purpose of a foundation?

You've probably never heard someone compliment the appearance of a foundation before. No one brags about the quality of a foundation. We don't stand around together dropping lines like, "You should see my foundation! It's the prettiest foundation you'll ever see."

Foundations aren't meant to be pretty or showy; they're meant to be foundational—sturdy, solid, stable, and strong. In fact, men only talk about foundations when a problem arises that needs to be looked at and addressed.

What happens when a building is constructed on top of a faulty foundation?

God crafted men with a foundation in mind. Your role here isn't to draw attention to yourself or be as showy as you can be. God has placed men in pivotal positions in order to provide the support, stability, and strength needed to build healthy communities and families.

As a kingdom man, God has given you a purpose to live out, a divine design to fulfill. This session speaks to your unique calling to provide the foundational framework upon which your influence can rest and rise.

Ask someone to pray before watching the video teaching.

Chosen for the Challenge

WATCH

Use this space to take notes during the video teaching.

MAN UP

Use the following questions to discuss the video teaching.

Read Genesis 18:19 together.

> *For I have chosen him, so that he may command his children and his household*
> *after him to keep the way of the LORD by doing righteousness and justice, so*
> *that the LORD may bring upon Abraham what He has spoken about him.*
>
> Genesis 18:19

Name some of the things God promised to Abraham.

When God called Abraham, He told him that He had chosen him. He promised to make Abraham's name great and his descendants many. He chose to bless Abraham in order to bless others (Gen. 12:1-3). God unleashed all of His promises upon Abraham so that ultimately, we might be blessed through our relationship with one of Abraham's descendants.

Read Galatians 3:29 together:

> *And if you belong to Christ, then you are Abraham's*
> *descendants, heirs according to promise.*
>
> Galatians 3:29

What did Paul mean when he wrote you were an heir of Abraham "according to promise"?

In what ways can Abraham's promises get passed down to you?

What responsibilities do we have because of the promises that have been given to us?

Every man is a draftee in the kingdom of God. Once we accept Jesus Christ, He lays claim to us, and that means we have a post to hold. You have a position to play on a bigger team. We've been given a blessing that God expects us to pass on to others. In other words, we're a part of a kingdom team. We've been called to take our stand with God, for God, from God, about God, in a world that needs to know God.

Why does following God compel us to take a stand for God?

Describe one way you have taken a stand for God recently. What did you learn from that experience? How others were impacted?

The blessing God gives us is meant to extend beyond us. One way to take a stand for God is to intentionally inject your life into the lives of other men. This is done through discipleship. When we disciple someone, we replicate the work of God in us to others who will then invest in others. Through discipleship God's creates a plethora of kingdom men with whom the world must contend.

What are some common hesitations men have when it comes to committing to disciple someone else or be discipled by someone else?

How do we sometimes rationalize "growing alone" in order to side-step the important calling of participating in discipleship?

Can you share a personal example of the result of having been discipled at some point in your life, or discipling someone else? If you do not have a personal example, share a hope you would expect to see as a result of men discipling other men.

PRAYER

Father, make us men who are intentional about standing up for You and fulfilling the role You have for us. Help us be men of our word who lives as a solid foundation of truth, wisdom and grace so that others around us can thrive. Open up opportunities for us to disciple other men, and to also be discipled as we seek to grow in spiritual maturity. In Christ's name, amen.

GOD'S MEET UP

Three times a year, God called the men of Israel to gather together and meet with Him through yearly festivals. Participating in the worship of God would define their identity and give them instructions for how to follow Him.

> *Three times a year all your males are to appear before the Lord*
> *GOD, the God of Israel. For I will drive out nations before you and*
> *enlarge your borders, and no man shall covet your land when you go*
> *up three times a year to appear before the LORD your God.*
>
> **Exodus 34:23-24**

God let the men know when they came before Him that if they were to follow His rules and come under His authority, then He would bless them, their families, and their nation. Specifically, God made three promises to protect them as the committed themselves to seeking the Lord. Let's take a deeper look at each of these three promises, and end each section with a couple of reflection questions for you to examine internally.

1
DRIVE OUT NATIONS BEFORE YOU

The promise to drive out nations before them was a promise of security. Enemy nations could only mean one thing: instability. While following God and seeking Him does not mean that our lives will always be easy, they will be secure in His grasp.

In what ways have you witnessed God bring stability and calm to your life as you follow Him?

Does stability from God mean that things around you are all stable too, or is it possible to be stable in an unstable circumstance? Explain why you answered as you did.

ENLARGE YOUR BORDERS

You have probably heard the term "enlarge your borders" in the familiar prayer of Jabez as well (1 Chron. 4:10). This is where a man named Jabez asked God to increase his influence. When God promises to enlarge a man's borders, He is referring to that space in which you carry influence and impact. This could be talking about your business, relationships, civic roles, or ministry.

Why might God extend the influence of those who are faithful to Him?

How could you spread God's goodness and rule in the places where God has given you impact?

ALLOW NO MAN TO COVET YOUR LAND

Sometimes it may not bother us if someone covets what we have. That's why so many of us post pictures of what we have and how we look on social media. A little bit of coveting, or admiration, can feel welcome to our flesh. In these verses God was making a promise that when these men left their homes to attend festivals no one would take what belonged to them. For you it means that you can trust God with all that He has entrusted to you.

Describe a time when you lost something you worked hard to achieve or acquire, and how that loss impacted your view of life.

Why is it important to rest in the truth of God's sovereign protection with regard to what He has given you? What is a consequence for those who do not rest in God's protection?

BIBLE STUDY 1
JUMP, OR BE JUMPED

When you purchase a game of checkers, you'll notice that on the top of each piece is the insignia of a crown. That is because each checker was created to become a king.

A checker is crowned because it has successfully made it to the other side of the board. After that point it will have the right and authority to maneuver and function at a much higher level than it could prior to being crowned. However, the reality is most individual checkers will not successfully make it to the other end of the board to be crowned, because the opposition will jump them and knock them out of the game. Whether a checker achieves its created goal of being crowned as a king is fully determined by the moves made by the hand controlling it.

When God created men, He created them with a crown because each man was made to rule under the authority of God. However, ever since the first man, Adam, Satan has sought to "jump" men to keep them from fulfilling their kingdom purposes. He goes to great lengths to keep us from functioning in alignment with God so that our families, churches, communities, and nation experience the consequences and confusion of men living independently of God. In the game of life, when it comes to spiritual warfare, you need to go on the offense. You will either need to jump, or you will be jumped by Satan's attacks.

Read 1 Peter 5:8-9 and Ephesians 4:26-27 and answer the following questions.

Be of sober spirit, be on the alert. Your adversary, the devil, prowls around like a roaring lion, seeking someone to devour. But resist him, firm in your faith, knowing that the same experiences of suffering are being accomplished by your brethren who are in the world.
1 Peter 5:8-9

Be angry, and yet to not sin; do not let the sun go down on your anger, and do not give the devil an opportunity.
Ephesians 4:26-27

What are some ways we can resist Satan's attempt to "jump" us?

Why do you think God allows Satan to prowl like a roaring lion, seeking men to devour?

Describe in your own words what it means to live with a "sober spirit" and always "on the alert" for Satan's schemes.

Satan is free to roam, within reason. God has Satan on a leash. Yet God will often allow Satan to tempt us as men, or wage warfare against us because it is in these times of testing that our true character is either formed or revealed.

The strength we need to successfully do battle with the devil is supplied by God (Eph. 6:10-11). That may seem obvious. But, judging from the way we treat this truth, it bears repeating.

Many of us tend to swing toward one of two extremes when it comes to the devil. Some men overestimate him. They become fearful and timid, lest Satan leap upon them. Others underestimate the devil. Yes, Satan is a defeated foe. But even though he is nothing more than a condemned death row inmate awaiting execution, it's not wise to sleep in his cell.

Mark your own perspective of Satan on the chart where 1 means you overestimate him and 10 means you underestimate him:

| 0 | 1 | 2 | 3 | 4 | 5 | 6 | 7 | 8 | 9 | 10 |

Why is it critical to have a healthy understanding of Satan's strategies and strengths in order to defeat him?

How should your understanding of Satan and his goals affect your decisions?

The inability to wage ongoing spiritual warfare over the enemy has kept too many men in a cycle of defeat, discouragement, confusion, rebellion, and addiction, to name a few.

As a result, we face the spiritual, social, racial, and political chaos we are experiencing today. Too many men have become either neutered and domesticated or abusive and irresponsible, creating a society that is torn, tattered, and in utter dysfunction.

Yet, despite all we see around us, there remains hope. If God can get His men to rise up as the kingdom men He has created us to be—men who pursue an intimate relationship with Him while simultaneously representing Him in all we do—He will reverse the downward spiral of the culture. God is waiting on His kingdom men to rise to the challenge we were chosen for and accept the responsibility of reversing the decay and disunity that engulf us.

Just as the first Adam brought defeat to the human race, the last Adam, Jesus Christ, came to bring victory (1 Cor. 15:22). It's time for God's men, under the lordship of Jesus Christ, to change the trajectory of our culture as we submit ourselves to Him and His kingdom agenda.

God's Kingdom Agenda is "the visible manifestation of the comprehensive rule of God over every area of life." Rephrase this in your own words.

Give an example of submitting yourself to Christ and His kingdom agenda.

How might your submission enable you to defeat the enemy's plans in your life?

If, and when, God's kingdom men decide to rise up to fulfill our calling, we will see God heal our hearts, families, churches, and land. We will see victory over Satan and his strategies. This study is a clarion call to those men who long to see what God will do with the awakening of His own disciples who will then lead their families and infiltrate the culture as kingdom citizens. Once we learn how to wage our own battles in order to wear our own crowns, we can then be used by God to crown the next generation with kingdom values as well. We were chosen for this challenge by God.

Why is it important for a society to have a shared set of values and standards passed down from one generation to another?

Read Judges 17:6 and answer the following questions.

In those days there was no king in Israel; every man
did what was right in his own eyes.
Judges 17:6

What happens to a culture when values are left up to everyone's interpretation?

How have you seen this happen in today's contemporary culture?

How has this kind of individualism damaged the spread of God's kingdom?

List one practical thing you can do this week in your sphere of influence in order to guide others toward God's set standards. (Be creative, this could mean in your family, at work, at church, on social media or also in your prayer time).

Pray about one area in your life where you need to step up your game against Satan's schemes. Look for what the Bible calls "opportunities," or open doors that Satan is using to break into your life. Ask God how you can close these doors to the enemy. Also spend some time in prayer asking for God's wisdom regarding His standard for society, families, and individual lives. Ask Him to reveal where your standards are not up to par with His own, so that you can adjust and be in alignment with God's will.

BIBLE STUDY 2
CALLED TO BE A KINGDOM MAN

A kingdom man may be defined as:

A man who visibly and consistently submits to the comprehensive relationship and rule of God, underneath the lordship of Jesus Christ, in every area of life.

You can sum it up in one short statement: A kingdom man accepts his responsibilities under God and faithfully carries them out. When he is faithful, God moves even pagan powers and other forces on earth to support him in doing his kingdom business. When he is unfaithful, Satan steals the show. God has called every Christian man to be a kingdom man.

Dr. Evans uses the word "consistently" in the definition of a kingdom man, rather than "perfectly." What does it look like to "consistently" live out a life of submission under God, especially in those times when you do fail or fall short?

Why is it spiritually dangerous to make excuses for your failures rather than accept responsibility for where you may have dropped the ball?

Consider a football team. When one player makes a mistake, it is common for that player to pat himself on his chest as a way of indicating that he knows it was his fault. It's a nonverbal way of saying, "Sorry guys, let's try again. That one was on me." The other players will nod or pat him on his shoulder and encourage him to do better next time. This type of honest awareness and self-evaluation allows teams to stay connected as a team while pursuing a shared goal. Our goal is consistency, not perfection.

How does personal ownership of failure or mishaps impact others?

In what ways can you take greater personal responsibility for mistakes or issues in your own family? In your friendships?

Have you ever worked with someone, or had a relationship with someone, who consistently blamed someone else for his or her own dropped balls? What did this pattern do to the relationships around them?

God calls each of us to own our failures and be authentic about our mistakes. Living as kingdom men requires submission which is consistency coupled with humility. This type of spirit creates an atmosphere of mutual respect, transparency, and grace where great things can be accomplished for God, individually and collectively.

Every man has been created by God with a specific post to fulfill and a purpose to live out. He has scouted, pursued, and drafted for His kingdom team. Our culture wants to give men a whole slew of other reasons for being a man, but God created men for greatness in His kingdom.

Read Genesis 18:17-19a and Galatians 3:16,29, then answer the following questions.

> *The LORD said, "Shall I hide from Abraham what I am about to do, since Abraham will surely become a great and mighty nation, and in him all the nations of the earth will be blessed? For I have chosen him …"*
> **Genesis 18:17-19a**

> *Now the promises were spoken to Abraham and to his seed. He does not say, "And to seeds," as referring to many, but rather to one, "And to your seed," that is, Christ.*
> **Galatians 3:16**

> *And if you belong to Christ, then you are Abraham's descendants, heirs according to promise.*
> **Galatians 3:29**

Describe how it makes you feel to know that you are truly an heir according to the promises given to Abraham.

How have you seen God bless others through you?

How would you like to see God bless others through you in the future?

Abraham's promise is ours through Jesus Christ. It's yours. Own it. Abraham's faith led to the blessing of untold millions for thousands of years after his death. Like Abraham, you are meant to pass your blessing onto others. To embrace God's promise naturally includes influencing all those around you. When you think of Tom Brady or Peyton Manning, you don't just think of somebody who played football. You think of someone who influenced the entire game of football, and their team. Why? Because they left their mark. Their mere presence elevated the players around them, and as a result, all were able to achieve more individually and collectively than many thought they ever would. We are to do the same.

Describe someone you know who "influences" and "elevates" the lives of others simply by who he is and what he does.

How can you position yourself to be used by God more so in "elevating" the lives of those within your sphere of influence to a greater degree?

I realize that many of you who have decided to participate in this Bible study may be at a place where you have made mistakes, you live with regret, or you have simply failed to maximize the gifts and skills God has given you. It could be that life hasn't been fair. You may want to embrace God's calling on your life, but you just don't know how you could possibly get there with all that is missing or messed up in your life.

If that's you, I want to remind you that success from God's perspective has more to do with heart than skill, just as success in football has more to do with effort than talent. Those who put in the work rise to the top. Those who arrive early and stay late create the historic stories with their games. Those who don't allow personal disadvantages to play out as disadvantages are the ones we later refer to as legends.

Tom Brady didn't get drafted until the sixth round but he went on to win, ironically enough, six Super Bowl championships (at the time of this writing.) Brady didn't allow what people thought of him—by choosing him lower on the rung—determine the effort he puts in the game. This principle ought to ring true for kingdom men too. It is your willingness to show up in life day in and day out, be present in relationships, put forth the effort on the job, commit, give, apply diligence, study the Word, invest in others, and the like that will shape your own legacy of distinction. God loves to use those who want to be used by Him. He consistently blesses those who consistently pursue Him.

Show up. Be present. Stay consistent.

If you do those three things, you will leave a legacy of excellence. After all, legacy is the culmination of a million middle moments done well. It's not about that Hail Mary or kickoff return for a touchdown. It's the small things—the consistent conversations and wise choices that add up over time. That's what creates the heritage you leave behind.

Dr. Evans describes legacy as "the culmination of a million middle moments done well." What practical steps can you take this week to focus more on the "middle moments" of life and investing in those around you?

Men, each of you are called to a life of greatness and purpose in God's kingdom. But greatness is created day in and day out when you show up and invest in the lives of others. It also requires that you be diligent in keeping your own spiritual muscles strong by seeking God above all else and embracing the calling and promises in His Word.

Pray for the discipline you need to live consistently as a kingdom man. Ask God to provide the structure in your life that will enable you to focus more fully on Him and His call for you. If you are in need of encouragement, take a moment to look around you and consider the impact you have had on others, for good and God's kingdom. If you are unable to recognize anything, ask the Spirit to reveal it to you. Then, build on that success every moment of every day moving forward.

The hand of the LORD was upon me, and He brought me out by the Spirit of the LORD and set me down in the middle of the valley; and it was full of bones. He caused me to pass among them round about, and behold, there were very many on the surface of the valley; and lo, they were very dry. He said to me, "Son of man, can these bones live?" And I answered, "O Lord God, You know."

EZEKIEL 37:1-3

WEEK 2
DRY BONES DANCING

START

Welcome to group session 2 of *Kingdom Men Rising.*

Last week we talked about being chosen for the challenge to live as a kingdom man. We saw the kind of man God wants for us to be and were challenged to extend our influence and impact for the glory of God.

Share one way you were encouraged by last week's session.

This week we will learn to overcome Satan's distractions and trust in God's plans, purposes, and promises for us.

Describe a strategy home-team fans use to distract the opposing team when they're trying to make a call to run a plan.

In what ways does Satan seek to use this same strategy to keep men from hearing clearly from God?

When an opposing team takes to the field in football, the home team fans will often yell loudly in order to keep the opposing team from hearing the play being called. In this way, they seek to disrupt the play and, essentially, become what is termed the "twelfth player" on the team.

Satan uses a similar strategy in our lives by keeping static on the line or inserting distractions into our hearts and minds so that we cannot hear clearly from God. Due to this effective approach, too many men remain down when they should be up, defeated when they should be winning, and lost when they should know the way to go. But God is calling to each of us loudly and clearly. It is up to us to focus, clear the static, and tune in to what He has to say.

Ask someone to pray before watching the video teaching.

Dry Bones Dancing

WATCH

Use this space to take notes during the video teaching.

MAN UP

Use the following questions to discuss the video teaching.

When you leave your town, and go to another town, if you have on a local radio signal, you're going to lose contact the further you get away from home. But when you come back, you'll pick up that signal again, because you're coming home.

Read Isaiah 64:4.

> *For from days of old they have not heard or perceived by ear, Nor has the eye seen a God besides You, Who acts in behalf of the one who waits for Him.*
> Isaiah 64:4

Why do you think those who did not hear, as referenced in Isaiah 64:4, could not discern or perceive God's voice?

In what ways is this lack of hearing evident in our culture today?

How does proximity to God increase our ability to hear from Him?

Far too many men have left home. We've left our commitment to God and have committed to our culture instead. Yet we still wonder why we're in a dry place, and we're not picking up heaven's signal anymore. To hear from heaven we need to leave the dry place far away from home and trust in the God who breathes life where there appears to be none.

> *The hand of the LORD was upon me, and He brought me out by the Spirit of the LORD and set me down in the middle of the valley; and it was full of bones. He caused me to pass among them round about, and behold, there were very many on the surface of the valley; and lo, they were very dry. He said to me, "Son of man, can these bones live?" And I answered, "O Lord GOD, You know."*
> Ezekiel 37:1-3

When Ezekiel was faced with the question of can these dry bones live, he gave the answer many men need to give today—"God, only You know. I can't answer that question because stuff looks so bad, and we're in such a mess, and things are so divided, and the chaos is so overwhelming." In other words, if this is going to be fixed, God has to fix it.

What areas of our culture today—either the church culture or the culture at large—appear to be beyond fixing from a human perspective?

Describe a time where you felt like you had no solution to the problem at hand, and yet you witnessed God come through to turn it around.

The account of Ezekiel and the dry bones lying dead on the valley floor reflects what many men sense in their lives during trials and difficulties. They feel like there is no way out of their slumber, struggling, and stumbling. Yet God will do everything He has purposed and promised in His Word

If we're going to become the men God has created us to be, we have to trust God's power. God has spoken and He has not stuttered. When we trust Him and embrace the promises from His Word, He can redeem any difficulty and cause the dry bones of our dire circumstances to get up and dance again.

If we have God's promises and know God's power, why do we often fail to trust them when life gets difficult?

What promises of God do you believe men need to trust in today?

What promises do you need to trust in personally?

PRAYER

Father, make us men who hear You clearly. Remove the static from the line so that we can discern Your voice. Help us identify the distractions in our lives that are keeping us from truly turning to You and understanding the truths You've outlined for us in Your Word. In Christ's name, amen.

HIT THE STREETS

GOD'S WORD AND SPIRIT

Take a moment to consider how to prevent another malfunction in the Soyuz MS-10 rocket which failed to reach the International Space Station in October, 2018. Get as detailed in your solution as you need to be.

To be honest, that was a trick question. Because it's hard to fix a problem when you don't know the cause. Whenever you are looking for a cure, you must address the cause. Far too many laymen, pastors, and politicians are doing patchwork on symptoms rather than dealing with the systemic roots that have led to the decay in our lives, families, communities, and nation. If we are ever to get things right, we have to address the spiritual causes beneath the brokenness we are experiencing.

God has given us two key methods for curing what ails us. He has provided two critical components we must apply in order to rise up from the ashes of decay. Both of these principles were given to Ezekiel when he stood in the valley of dead, dry bones. They are: 1) Return to God's Word, and 2) Receive a fresh encounter with God's Spirit.

1 RETURN TO GOD'S WORD.

Again He said to me, 'Prophesy over these bones and say to them, 'O dry bones, hear the word of the LORD.' Thus says the Lord GOD to these bones, 'Behold, I will cause breath to enter you that you may come to life.

Ezekiel 37:4-5

Men, if you're dry—spiritually, emotionally, relationally, or in any other way—it is most likely because you are distant from God and His Word. Spending regular and unhurried time in God's Word is essential for spiritual life and growth.

When will you spend time with God daily? Draft a battle plan below. Set a time and a place. Write down your approach here.

Just as a computer system can only work off of the information inputted into it, your mind and heart needs the insertion of God's Word in order to utilize it. What method can you apply to memorize God's Word?

2 RECEIVE A FRESH ENCOUNTER WITH GOD'S SPIRIT.

Then He said to me, "Prophesy to the breath, prophesy, son of man, and say to the breath, 'Thus says the Lord GOD, 'Come from the four winds, O breath, and breathe on these slain, that they come to life.'" So I prophesied as He commanded me, and the breath came into them, and they came to life and stood on their feet, an exceedingly great army."

Ezekiel 37:9-10

After the truth of His Word was given to the dry bones in the valley, God then gave them the power of His Spirit. The original Hebrew word translated as "breath" in verse nine is the word God used to identify His Spirit at the beginning of the creation process in Genesis 1:2. With His Spirit, God breathed new life into the dead bones. Through this combination of the Word and the Spirit, God awakened lifeless bones.

How does the Holy Spirit awaken and invigorate God's work in you?

List three practical ways you can connect more authentically with the Holy Spirit. Seek to apply these three ways every day this week, and then come back and describe what impact that had on your life.

BIBLE STUDY 1
INTIMACY WITH AN IMAGE

A few years ago, I received a phone call from a friend who felt hopeless. His life had taken a turn for the worse, and he saw no way out. I tried to remind him about God's ability to make a way out of no way and encouraged him to keep his eyes on Christ. But the more we talked, the stronger the resolution to remain hopeless came through in his voice. The next day I learned my friend had taken his life.

This wasn't the first person I knew who had taken their life, but this one hit me particularly hard. I wondered if I could have said something different to make him change his mind. The weight of his words and the faintness of his voice hung heavy over me for a very long time. Hopelessness is a terrible thing because it means you have given up on the future. You've thrown in the towel. Far too many men today are living in hopelessness.

You see this hopelessness when men walk away from their responsibilities to their families, to their communities, or their church. You see this hopelessness when they no longer believe that God can make a difference in history. This hopelessness manifests itself in a culture rife with conflict and division. You may wonder, "Why?" Why did God allow this to get this bad? I have discovered that God has a way of letting life get so low until the only way you can look is up. In Ezekiel, we see God's judgment poured out on a culture filled with impurity and idol worship.

Read the Scripture below and answer the following questions.

> *Then the word of the LORD came to me saying, "Son of man, when the house of Israel was living in their own land, they defiled it by their ways and their deeds; their way before Me was like the uncleanness of a woman in her impurity. Therefore I poured out My wrath on them for the blood which they had shed on the land, because they had defiled it with their idols.*
> **Ezekiel 36:16-18**

In what ways is God's judgment evident in societies and cultures today?

Read Proverbs 3:11-12. Why does God discipline us in response to disobedience? vWhy is this actually good for us?

In Ezekiel's day and in our own, the world is filled with idols. Simply explained, idolatry is intimacy with an image. It's not necessarily bowing down to a carved statue stuck on a pole. An idol is anything that usurps God's rightful rule in your life. Idols come in all shapes and sizes. What's more, they can even be found in the church. Idolatry centers on alignment—you align your thoughts, words, and actions under what you value most.

What are some modern day idols we esteem in our culture?

Making this more personal, what is an idol you struggle to place in its proper position under God?

What steps do you need to take to remove this idol and realign your life under God's rule?

Idolatry manifests itself in lifestyle choices that are contrary to God's expressed will in His inerrant Word. Consider what Paul says in his letter to the church at Colossae.

> *Therefore consider the members of your earthly body as dead to immorality, impurity, passion, evil desire, and greed, which amounts to idolatry.*
> **Colossians 3:5**

What are some ways idolatry becomes evident in the choices we make? In what way does greed manifest as idolatry in a person's life?

How should knowing that greed and impurity are considered idols by God affect the way you approach both?

Clinging to idols is forsaking the faithfulness of God. When the pendulum of our hearts swings towards idolatry, it slides away from God's love and power. However the opposite is also true. When we forsake idols our heart swings into alignment with God's grace, faithfulness, power and love in our lives. To embrace God's will and activate the flow of His love and power into our lives, we must turn away from idols. God has made it clear, through His Word, how to activate the flow of His love and power into your life, as well as how to deactivate it.

Turning away from common cultural temptations like impurity, evil desires, greed, pride, and selfishness enables you to open up the floodgate of God's love, favor and blessing in your life. Idolatry is the number one factor in most of life's difficulties and disasters. Until we identify the root of idolatry and deal with it by removing it from our hearts, we cannot expect a different outcome.

Read Ezekiel 37:14. What power has God given to help you uncover and remove idols?

Describe a time when God removed a sinful pattern from your life, or in someone's life whom you know.

What did it take to root out the idols?

God has given us the means and the method for removing the idols that grip our hearts. Through the Holy Spirit, He has given us new life in the Spirit which provides the means to diagnose and dismiss our idols.

When God speaks of the resurrection in the Book of Ezekiel, it ultimately points us to Christ who has conquered sin, death, and the grave. Through Jesus, we have been given the power of the Holy Spirit (the new Spirit God promised in Ezekiel, and His life inside of us helps us put to death the idols our flesh leads us to pursue. Prayer and self-evaluation provide the methods for us to begin uprooting idols and casting them aside.

Describe what it means to "put to death" that which belongs to your earthly nature.

How does removing our idols free us to glorify God?

Read Psalm 139:23-24. Why is it essential for men to pause and take inventory of their heart and lives regularly?

How does prayer contribute to spiritual growth?

Prayer lets us communicate directly with God. As we bring our request, God begins to direct the thoughts and intentions of our hearts. We hear from Him and invite Him to put to death what is earthly in us. Let's end our time today by taking advantage of God's means and method for dealing with idolatry.

> Pray about one area in your life that needs to be "put to death" in order that it can be raised again according to God's Word and by His power. Ask God to draw your attention to what this is and how you can honor Him by letting it go and ridding its hold on your heart. Then, seek God's wisdom on what you can do to replace that gap in your life in a healthy, loving, and productive way.

BIBLE STUDY 2
A KEY WITHOUT A CAR

Imagine for a moment that someone handed you the keys to a brand new Lamborghini. The keys were all yours, they said. But the car was nowhere to be found. In fact, when you asked where the car was, all you were told is, "Somewhere." Fast forward a few weeks and, despite looking for the car for days on end, you still have not found the car. At that point in time, how valuable are those keys?

Most people would answer that question, "Not very valuable at all." This is because keys—on their own—won't do you any good. Keys need to be coupled with a car to understand their true value.

Similarly, all of us have access to Bibles, whether it's a physical copy or an app on your phone. But in order to unlock the true value of God's Word, we must commit to reading and applying it. Both pieces are necessary. God's Word must be understood and applied in order for it to activate God's power in your life.

Why is it spiritually dangerous to read God's Word without applying it to your life?

God's Word does not work just because you get excited about it when you read it. It doesn't work just because you heard a sermon or a podcast and got all fired up. It doesn't even work because you spent some time thinking about it or posted a verse on social media. It doesn't work because you could ace Bible trivia. All of those things are nice. But if it's not applied, you won't get to experience the fullness of what God's Word is meant to do. To listen to God's Word but refuse to act on it causes a man to do little more than waste his life.

Often when God does spectacular things in the Bible, He asks His people to first take a step of obedience. Read the following verses and describe the common theme throughout..

As for you, lift up your staff and stretch out your hand over the sea and divide it, and the sons of Israel shall go through the midst of the sea on dry land.
Exodus 14:16

It shall come about when the soles of the feet of the priests who carry the ark of the LORD, the Lord of all the earth, rest in the waters of the Jordan, the waters of the Jordan will be cut off, and the waters which are flowing down from above will stand in one heap.
Joshua 3:13

We read before Lazarus was raised from the dead:

Jesus said, "Remove the stone."
John 11:39a

List the simple steps of faith that preceded God's miraculous work in the verses you just read.

Why do you think God often uses our obedience to bring about the power of His Word in our lives?

Describe the difference between awareness of God's Word and obedience.

Without faith, obedience, and application hearing God's Word is just knowledge acquisition. Simply hearing the Word then moving on with life as if nothing has or should change will never produce the supernatural intervention of God in your circumstances. Hearing, believing, and doing the Word of God is the foundation of wisdom.

Wisdom is both the ability and the responsibility of applying God's truth to life's choices. You can only identify a wise man or a fool by his decisions. We feel like dry bones wasting away because we haven't sought God's wisdom to bring about a different result. Godly wisdom sets men on a path out of the valley of sin.

Read James' teaching on wisdom.

This wisdom is not that which comes down from above, but is earthly, natural, demonic. For where jealousy and selfish ambition exist, there is disorder and every evil thing. But the wisdom from above is first pure, then peaceable, gentle, reasonable, full of mercy and good fruits, unwavering, without hypocrisy. And the seed whose fruit is righteousness is sown in peace by those who make peace.

James 3:15-18

What is the difference between earthly and godly wisdom?

In what ways can you develop and strengthen your ability to apply godly wisdom to your everyday decisions?

Have you ever experienced a time where you tried to merge human thoughts with God's wisdom? What was the result?

God created you for more than you can ever imagine. But often we miss out on all that God can or will do through us because we pursue the wisdom of the world rather than the wisdom of God. Looking back to our illustration, we're the man standing in an empty garage holding the keys but not knowing what to do with them.

To embrace all that God has for you, you have to interact with His Word and His Spirit so that His Spirit can bring the wisdom of His Word to your heart and mind. That means more than just reading and knowing the Bible. You have to act on what it says (see Jas. 2:26). The power of God's promises remains dormant unless activated by your faith.

Pursuing godly wisdom brings "good fruits." In other words, godly wisdom produces results. Embracing wisdom means we are obeying and applying God's truth to our lives. God is waiting on you to take your rightful place in this world. He is waiting for you to rise to the occasion and secure your spot of significance in His kingdom made manifest on earth. But that happens when you step out—fully, faithfully, and single-mindedly—according to the direction of His will.

In what way does God want to you to apply His Word in a more proactive way to life's choices?

How would you advise someone who is new to studying God's Word on how to find His wisdom on a specific subject? If you do not know what you would say, consider doing an Internet search on some helpful tips, then writing them down to share with others.

Where is God calling on you to seek His wisdom? What area of life do you need a deeper understanding of His Word?

God is not going to force His wisdom on you. You have to discern it and then apply it. He has given each of us the free will to make our own choices, for good or for bad. But He has also given us the ability to ask Him for wisdom on how to make the best possible choices in whatever situation we face (Jas. 1:5).

Pray for God's wisdom on how to know His Word better, understand it more fully and apply it more diligently in your life. Ask Him to reveal to you those areas in the past where you have gotten off track from applying His truth to your choices. Once these are revealed, ask for His forgiveness and guidance on how to restore what has been broken or damaged due to those decisions. Then seek to obey Him in what He reveals to you to do. With His help, He can revive anything in your life that seems beyond redemption. But, remember, it requires your participation in the process.

But Peter said, "I do not possess silver and gold, but what I do have I give to you: In the name of Jesus Christ the Nazarene— walk!" And seizing him by the right hand, he raised him up; and immediately his feet and his ankles were strengthened.

ACTS 3:6-7

WEEK 3
GET UP

START

Welcome to group session 3 of *Kingdom Men Rising.*

Last session, we considered how God's Word brings purpose and direction to our lives. We saw how God can take a stale or declining spiritual life and make it live again like Ezekiel saw in the valley of dry bones.

Describe one meaningful truth from last session with the group.

This week we're going to be talking about how to get up and overcome what is holding us back.

In what ways are men able to help other men to get up after they have been knocked down?

I'm sure you have seen it if you have watched any sports at all. The game is going on like normal then a player goes down. The team gathers around the player as the medics rush to his side. Some teammates drop to a knee. Others stand quietly nearby, trying to listen to how bad the injury might be.

If the medic doesn't signal for the cart, another familiar scene often takes place as well. That's when the medic or another player will come alongside of the injured player and help him off the field. He will extend a hand to help him get up and off to the sidelines.

Sometimes life's difficulties knock us out, beat us down, or get us off the field completely. But there are other times, when a helpful friend can go a long way in getting us back on our feet and in the game again. Standing up after you've been knocked down is rarely a solo experience. It takes others to come alongside you to lift you, encourage you, and strengthen you until you can once again stand on your own.

Ask someone to pray before watching the video teaching.

Get Up

WATCH

Use this space to take notes during the video teaching.

Video sessions available at Lifeway.com/KingdomMenRising or with a subscription to SmallGroup.com

MAN UP

Use the following questions to discuss the video teaching.

Read Acts 3:1-2 together.

Now Peter and John were going up to the temple at the ninth hour, the hour of prayer. And a man who had been lame from his mother's womb was being carried along, whom they used to set down every day at the gate of the temple which is called Beautiful, in order to beg alms of those who were entering the temple.

Acts 3:1-2

This verse gives a stark contrast in the location the lame man sat down each day to beg and his own life situation. Luke, the author of Acts, specifically lets us as readers know that the gate was called "Beautiful."

What kind of hardship do you imagine this man dealt with day after day?

Why does suffering, physical or otherwise, often impact our spiritual lives?

Much of the lameness we experience in our own lives comes about through comparison. Comparing yourself to others can have a crippling effect on what you do. If you ever see two quarterbacks competing for the same role, they will often underperform. This is because they know they are being scrutinized and compared. Yet when a franchise shows confidence in one quarterback and assures him of his role, he will regularly play with a higher level of competence.

Describe some of the ways men limit their own potential by comparing themselves to others.

How does comparison often lead to emotional pain and hardship?

Lameness comes in all shapes and sizes. We can be lame emotionally. We can be lame spiritually, where we're so far from God's perspective that we lean to our own understanding. We can be lame morally, not making the right choices, abusing women, and also abusing ourselves. We can be lame relationally because we're hanging out with the wrong people, doing the wrong things. We can be lame in our careers, feeling like we are failures. And we fake it, we pretend that we can stand up and man up. We use all the words, but still we can't stand on our own two feet. And that makes us like this man in Acts 3, a "spiritual beggar."

What does it look like to be a "spiritual beggar"?

We all enter the kingdom of heaven poor in spirit (see Matt. 5:3). At some point we have to get up from the ground get healed and get help. Then we can help other spiritual beggars rise up to be the men God created them to be. Once the lame man was healed, he got up and started praising God (Acts 4:8). The power of God became active in his life, and he returned the praise to God.

What specific, practical steps can you take this week to overcome any personal spiritual lameness in your life?

Now consider who needs your help. What specific, practical steps can you take this week to help someone else overcome any personal spiritual lameness in his life?

PRAYER

Father, You have charged us with the calling of rising as kingdom men. It is not okay to stay down, defeated, and bound by any emotional or spiritual strongholds. We ask that You shine a light onto those areas in our lives where we need to heal, grow, and become stronger. Give us the humility we need to ask others for help. Give us the wisdom we need to help others who can benefit from our help. In Jesus' name, amen.

HIT THE STREETS

STAND TALL AND TELL OTHERS

Just like our bodies can experience muscle atrophy due to poor nutrition or a lack of use, our spiritual life can deteriorate when we give up or throw in the towel due to difficulties we face. But God gives us four key principles, based on the story of the lame man, which we can apply in order to overcome spiritual and emotional lameness. We find these in Acts 3:

> And he began to give them his attention, expecting to receive something from them. But Peter said, "I do not possess silver and gold, but what I do have I give to you: In the name of Jesus Christ the Nazarene—walk!" And seizing him by the right hand, he raised him up; and immediately his feet and his ankles were strengthened. With a leap he stood upright and began to walk; and he entered the temple with them, walking and leaping and praising God.
>
> Acts 3:5-8

GIVE GOD YOUR ATTENTION

The first step you must take to restoring spiritual strength when it has been lost is to turn your attention to God. Like the lame man begging at the temple, expect to receive something. What God gives you may be different from what you expect to get, but that doesn't rid you of your personal responsibility to look to Him with hope.

RECEIVE HIS HELP

God's help can come to you in any number of ways. It may come through a friend, a book, a sermon, a small group, a coach, or a pastor or mentor. However God chooses to send you the guidance and wisdom you need on the path to your spiritual restoration, it is up to you to receive it. No one is going to do it all for you. Participate in the process of your own healing.

3 STAND ON YOUR OWN

Once God gives you what you need in order to be lifted from the slump of spiritual lameness, be willing to stand on your own. Take responsibility for your next step. Do not allow yourself to become so dependent upon others that you fail to realize and utilize your own strength. Muscles develop as you use them. The same is true for the spiritual and emotional life. You may only go so far on your own at the start, but with time, you will increase your distance.

4 PRAISE GOD AND TELL OTHERS

As God continues to strengthen you and rebuild the parts of your life that were broken, do not keep it to yourself. Show others what He has done in your life. Demonstrate to others what is possible. In this way, you encourage others in their own healing as well. As you praise God and tell of His power, you create a ripple effect of personal growth in others too.

Which of the principles do you need to embrace right now?

What might that look like for you? Be specific.

PARTICIPATE IN THE PROCESS

Have you ever gotten a card for your birthday and you opened the envelope but you didn't even read the card, you just shook the card? You did this because you wanted to know if the person who sent you the card had given you any greenbacks in your card. Or, maybe, did they write a check? If you were to be honest, you would admit that you don't even care that much about the card. You care about what's in the card!

You and I both know how disappointing it is on your birthday to only get a card with nothing in it. Well, you can imagine how disappointed the lame man was in Acts 3 when Peter told him that he didn't have any silver or gold to give him. Especially since they had stopped in response to his begging. When you stop, that usually means you're going to do something.

Sometimes delays are good for us. God has a habit of delaying His provision and intervention in our lives for a greater purpose. One of the purposes is to be sure He has our full attention first.

Read Psalm 62:1 and Psalm 69:3 then answer the following questions.

My soul waits in silence for God only;
From Him is my salvation.
Psalm 62:1

I am weary with my crying; my throat is parched;
My eyes fail while I wait for my God.
Psalm 69:3

Why would God delay His help and cause us to wait on Him?

How does being asked to wait on God heighten our spiritual sensitivities to what He is about to do?

Describe a time when God didn't give you what you desired at the time, but He came through at a later date. What did the waiting teach you about God? About yourself?

The lame man from Acts 3 was taken to the gate of the temple every day (v. 2). Even though this was an area with heavy foot traffic, he was likely ignored. As Peter and John walked by the lame man, Peter said, "Look at us!" (v. 4) Now, if Peter had to tell him to "look at us," that means he wasn't looking at them to begin with. That gives us great insight into this lame man. Peter needed this man's undivided attention. He needed him to focus. He needed him to hear him. If this man truly wanted a solution, he'd need to pay close attention to Peter right then. He needed to be part of the solution.

Healing and empowerment are not a one-way gift through the touch of a magic wand. True healing requires your desire, responsibility, and focus. That's why Jesus would often ask the question "Do you want to be made well?" He didn't just walk around tapping people on the head, bestowing health and healing on whomever was near. Keep in mind, crowds of people flocked around Jesus wherever He went. Lines formed. Inevitably people walked away unhealed. Rather, Jesus would ask if the person was willing to be made whole. Healing and wholeness come in a process of belief and through a desire to be made well.

How does our personal participation in the process of healing lead to deeper growth?

How does our participation help us understand those seasons where God asks or expects us to wait on His timing?

Physical therapists can do wonders with patients who want to be made well. But if a patient does not have the will to get better, the improvements are typically less drastic, if any at all. Oftentimes, a physical therapist will notate on a patient's chart that the patient is either "noncompliant" or "noncooperative." This lets the other nurses or therapists gain insight into why the progression toward wholeness is moving so slowly.

When God restores the parts of us that have been damaged by sin or wounded through personal neglect or harm, He wants our cooperation in the process. Without it, long-term progress cannot take place.

In what ways can a person cooperate with God in the process of healing from spiritual lameness or emotional wounds?

In what ways can a person resist God, or the help of others, in the process of personal growth? What is often the result?

Just like it is rare for a man to lift a large amount of weights alone in a gym, without a spotter or someone to encourage and help, growth in the spiritual life does not happen in a silo. We are all part of a collective process, cooperating with God and others in our healing and spiritual development. Our willingness to experience life more intimately with others and more humbly before God will have a large impact on how much lameness we are able to overcome, both individually and as a group. We cannot be content with past victories, we must continue to participate in our faith journey as Paul wrote in Philippians 2.

> *So then, my beloved, just as you have always obeyed, not as in my presence only,*
> *but now much more in my absence, work out your salvation with fear and trembling*
> *for it is God who is at work in you, both to will and to work for His good pleasure.*
> **Philippians 2:12-13**

On a scale of 0-10, how much effort do you put into your own spiritual healing and growth?

0   1   2   3   4   5   6   7   8   9   10

What makes it difficult for you to invest more than you do?

On a scale of 0-10, how much effort does God put into your spiritual healing and growth (both to will and to work for His good pleasure)?

0   1   2   3   4   5   6   7   8   9   10

Are you willing to cooperate with God on a greater level so that He can develop and unleash you to do His kingdom work?

What practical steps can you take to participate more intentionally in your own personal path to spiritual maturity, strength, healing and growth?

Who is another more mature kingdom man who can help you get up from the ground when you're down and in need of spiritual strength and healing?

> Pray about your willingness to participate in the process of healing, helping, and growing as men. Ask God to reveal where you have been unwilling to either lend a hand, or receive a hand, toward greater spiritual maturity. Seek ways you can become better connected with other men so that iron can truly sharpen iron as Scripture says it should (Prov. 27:17).

DO YOU KNOW WHAT YOU KNOW?

A POW is a prisoner of war—a person who has been captured by the enemy and is held hostage during conflict. The opposing forces control the prisoner's living conditions, activities, and movements. Many men live like POWs, but rather than being prisoners of war, they're prisoners of addictive behavior. They have been captured by the enemy, and there appears to be no way of escape. They feel trapped in situations and circumstances that the world labels as addiction. Drugs, sex, pornography, alcohol, relationships, negative self-talk, work, food, gambling, spending—these things become coping mechanisms for life's pain, disappointments, and boredom. When an action or activity begins to influence you more than you influence it, it can leave you feeling trapped.

I sometimes compare addictive behavior to quicksand. The harder you try to get out of a situation, the deeper you sink. Human methods can never set you free from a spiritual stranglehold on your life. Rather, these attempts will make you sink faster.

Another problem that arises when someone is sinking in quicksand involves focus. Remember when Peter stepped off the boat to walk to Jesus on the waves (Matt. 14:22-23)? Things were going great, then his vision for circumstances overtook his focus on Christ. Where you look matters. If a person stares only at the sand surrounding them, they will miss the stick being held out to them that they must grasp to be dragged out. We rely on human methods when only spiritual methods can deliver.

Consider Paul's words about our the conflict going on all around us.

> For though we walk in the flesh, we do not war according to the flesh, for
> the weapons of our warfare are not of the flesh, but divinely powerful
> for the destruction of fortresses. We are destroying speculations and
> every lofty thing raised up against the knowledge of God, and we
> are taking every thought captive to the obedience of Christ.
>
> **2 Corinthians 10:4-5**

What must happen first in order for us to overcome a stronghold in our life?

Have you ever attempted to overcome a stronghold of the flesh by using the flesh? What was the result?

One reason strongholds are so powerful is that they're so entrenched. They become entrenched when we buy into the lie that our situation is hopeless. His goal is to get you to believe that by nature you are a drug addict or a manipulator or a negative person, that you are controlled by fear or shame, that nothing will ever change. Once you adopt this line of thinking, these unhelpful patterns become entrenched fortresses that are difficult to remove. As a result, your behavior deteriorates even more because we always act according to who we believe we are.

The only solution is to tear down these fortresses by "taking every thought captive to the obedience of Christ." This means to replace your harmful and untrue thoughts with the better promises of God. Embracing this advice from Scripture reprograms your mind and releases you from spiritual strong holds. You become free yourself so then you can help other men rise to do the same.

Why is it important to reprogram your mind in order to break free from a spiritual or emotional stronghold?

Name some common cultural influences that can be used by the enemy to keep your mind hearing, rehearsing and believing the lies of this world.

What thoughts do you need to take captive?

Overcoming personal strongholds is a two-part process of reprogramming your mind. First, identify Christ's thoughts on a matter, and secondly, align your own thinking under the rule of His truth. The truth, then, will set you free (John 8:32). Let's work through this process together.

Reflect on a particular struggle you have, then answer the following questions.

Write out your thoughts on this struggle. Be specific.

What promises of Christ speak to this struggle? Get your Bible or Bible app and find specific Scriptures that speak to your struggle.

Identify the ways your thinking is out of alignment with Christ's thoughts.

How must you adjust your thoughts to align under the rule of Christ's truth?

Keep in mind that just acknowledging the truth won't break any bonds. John 8:32 says that you "will know" the truth and then be set free. The word for "will know" in the original Greek of the New Testament is a verb that literally means both "to know" and "to be known." The word refers not to head knowledge, but deep and intimate familiarity with a subject. It is the same word used in Matthew 1:25 (NKJV) when the Scripture says that Joseph did not know (have sexual relations with) Mary while she was pregnant. The NASB says that he "kept her a virgin until she gave birth to a Son." The literal translation of in Matthew 1:25 is "and was not knowing her."

To know the truth, in the biblical form of this word, is to make it an intrinsic part of who you are. It is to know and be known by it, in the deepest, most authentic place in you. To know ourselves in this way, we need to be in a constant relationship with the Scriptures.

> *For the word of God is living and active and sharper than any two-edged*
> *sword, and piercing as far as the division of soul and spirit, of both joints*
> *and marrow, and able to judge the thoughts and intentions of the heart.*
> **Hebrews 4:12**

Describe the difference between "knowing" something cognitively and "knowing" something intimately? Why is this important when it comes to knowing God's Word?

How has God's Word freed you from hardship and sin in the past?

As you seek to heal from any and every spiritual and emotional stronghold you may face, or as you seek to guide other men into healing as well, be sure to identify what Christ says on the matter, and then memorize it, meditate on it, and apply it. It is not enough to simply be aware of the truth. Just like it is not enough to simply be aware of your dinner. You must consume your dinner for it to have any positive impact on your body. Similarly, you must consume the Word of God in such a way that it becomes an intrinsic part of your nature on a regular basis.

Pray for God to inspire you to know His Word on a deeper level. Invite Him to show you ways you can discover truth in His Word beyond what you have done in the past. Ask Him to connect you with other men who have a similar hunger for His Word. In this way, you can grow together and strengthen each other as you rise together as kingdom men.

The angel of the LORD appeared to him and said to him, "The LORD is with you, O valiant warrior."

JUDGES 6:12

WEEK 4
GET GOING

START

Welcome to session 4 of *Kingdom Men Rising*.

Look back at your answers to the exercise on page 56. Would someone share how this exercise was helpful to them?

Last session Dr. Evans taught about getting up from your struggles. This week we talk about how to get going to move beyond the idols in our lives.

How does loyalty and commitment contribute to healthy relationships?

No man with an intention of marrying a woman he is dating will do what we often refer to as "two-time" her. To "two-time" is to date two different women at the same time. When a man desires to date and marry a specific woman, he makes sure his loyalty and commitment to her are known, and felt.

This is common sense to most men. But somehow we lose common sense when it comes to maintaining and cultivating our relationship with God. To "two-time" God is to set any competing interest at the same level as Him in our hearts. That could show up in a number of areas—entertainment, focus, relationships, addiction, money, and any number of things.

As we've already seen in this study, idolatry is intimacy with an image. We don't have to bow down to a carved statues to be idolaters. We worship idols when we allow anything to usurp God's rightful place in our lives.

Ask someone to pray before watching the video teaching.

WATCH

Use this space to take notes during the video teaching.

MAN UP

Use the following questions to discuss the video teaching.

Read Jonah 2:8 together.

Those who cling to worthless idols turn away from God's love for them.
Jonah 2:8, NIV

What does it mean to "cling" to an idol? How do idols cause us to "turn away from God's love" for us?

The number one sin in the Bible, second to none, is the sin of idolatry. From Genesis to Revelation, you will see God condemning idols. An idol is a "God substitute" or any noun—person, place, thing, or thought—that you look to as your source. Whenever anything becomes your source, it is an automatic idol. There are primitive idols that we may not identify with today. But then there are American idols. It can be materialism. It can be greed. It can be relationships. It can be sports. It can be your career because it's your source. And God will always judge idolatry.

In the video, Dr. Evans lists five idols that plague men. How can each of these things become idols that rob our affection for God?

Materialism:

Greed:

Relationships:

Sports:

Career:

How are the idols we just listed widely accepted by men today?

How can a sense of entitlement lead to idolatry?

Living with idols, as we read in Jonah 2:8, creates distance in our relationship with God. Like a two-timing man, our attention is divided between God and the idols we are pursuing. Far too many men are failing to advance in their careers as God had intended, or thrive in their homes and communities as they have been designed to do so because they have chosen to embrace idolatry in one form or another. Many pursue idols without even realizing what they're doing.

What do you think has contributed to a lack of awareness of how our personal choices lead us to idolatry?

What could be done to increase our awareness and ownership of how contemporary idols are harming our relationship with God and our culture?

Too many men today have identified with too many false gods. Men need to step up, get going, and move away from the lifeless idols robbing them of spiritual vitality and impact. When we put away our idols and embrace God's better plan for our lives, He will use us to do something bigger than what we could have ever done on our own.

In the teaching, Dr. Evans gave Gideon and Moses as examples of men God used beyond their limited human ability. How did God use these men? How did God overwhelm and overcome their limitations?

Describe a time in your life, or in the life of someone you know, when God's purpose or calling was bigger than what could be done on your own.

PRAYER

Father, remove from my heart any dependence or loyalty on anything I place higher than You. I confess any and all idolatry I have allowed in my life and I take full responsibility for having let it into my heart. Forgive me and show me a better way. Give me a "burning bush" experience and an encounter with You in order to guide me in a new direction of honoring You first and foremost in all I think, say, and do. In Christ's name, amen.

GOD GOES FIRST

In this session's video teaching, we are exploring the life of a man named Gideon. Gideon was a man of no reputation. He would not have been the first chosen in any backyard football game. And where Gideon lacked in known abilities, he equaled in a lack of confidence. Yet, God used Gideon in a mighty way in order to defeat a more powerful army who had held his people oppressed for far too long. How did Gideon rise up and become victorious? He learned that spiritual success in spiritual war depends entirely upon spiritual solutions.

Gideon first had to learn that God was His source. When we meet Gideon, he is fearful and timid. But God had other plans, as He often does. Gideon had to learn to see himself from God's viewpoint. Read the following verses that describe Gideon's call from God and consider the three principles we can learn from this account.

Then the angel of the LORD came and sat under the oak that was in Ophrah, which belonged to Joash the Abiezrite as his son Gideon was beating out wheat in the wine press in order to save it from the Midianites. The angel of the LORD appeared to him and said to him, "The LORD is with you, O valiant warrior." Then Gideon said to him, "O my lord, if the LORD is with us, why then has all this happened to us? And where are all His miracles which our fathers told us about, saying, 'Did not the LORD bring us up from Egypt?' But now the LORD has abandoned us and given us into the hand of Midian." The LORD looked at him and said, "Go in this your strength and deliver Israel from the hand of Midian. Have I not sent you?" He said to Him, "O Lord, how shall I deliver Israel? Behold, my family is the least in Manasseh, and I am the youngest in my father's house." But the LORD said to him, "Surely I will be with you, and you shall defeat Midian as one man."

Judges 6:11–16

1
GOD SEES OUR CIRCUMSTANCES CLEARLY

Gideon was overwhelmed with his circumstances because he failed to see that God was with him (vv. 11-13). The Midianites were fearsome enemies, but they were no match for God. As He brought Israel out of Egypt, He would deliver them from the Midianites. He was waiting on Gideon's participation.

2
GOD SEES A WARRIOR WHERE WE SEE A WIMP

God saw Gideon differently than Gideon saw himself. When God charged Gideon with a task, Gideon responded, "my family is the least in Manasseh, and I am the youngest in my father's house" (v. 15). While he thought he was a wimp, God knew he was a "valiant warrior" (v. 12). Gideon was so overwhelmed by His circumstances that He forgot how God saw him.

3
GOD SEES HIS ABILITY MORE THAN OUR LIMITATIONS

God told Gideon He was with Him (v. 12), that Gideon was a warrior (v. 12). Based on that truth, God sent Gideon on a mission—He told Gideon he would "defeat Midian as one man" (v. 16). Gideon only saw his ability instead of God's. For too long, he had trusted in idols rather than the God of Israel, but God was about to change all of that.

Rising up as a kingdom man requires alignment with God's plans and purposes. As we see from the passages above, as well as through the life of Gideon, God's presence produces the victory we seek. Yet one way we often remove God's presence from our lives is through the sin of idolatry. Gideon had to first tear down the idols in order to open the gap for God to move in his situation (Judg. 6:25-32).

Which of these principles is most meaningful to you?

Which do you need to take hold of right now?

BIBLE STUDY 1
USE WHAT HE GAVE YOU

We should not expect God to do something through us outside of our home or inner circle if we are not first willing to get things right within it. You may have heard me say it like this:

> *A messed-up man contributes to a messed-up family, which then contributes to a messed-up church. A messed-up church contributes to a messed-up community, which then contributes to a messed-up county. A messed-up county contributes to a messed-up state, which then contributes to a messed-up country. And a messed-up country contributes to a messed-up world. Therefore, if you want a better world comprising better countries made up of better states containing better counties populated by better communities housing better churches attended by better families, it starts off with being a better man. It starts with you. Right now. Right here.*

The deliverance of the entire nation of Israel from the hands of the Midianites started with one man seeking a better world. It started with Gideon, right in his own home. Before Gideon could ever take on a national enemy, he had to first tear down his family's idols. God had raised up Gideon for a mighty conquest but he had to demonstrate faithfulness first. Before God would bless Gideon's work, He asked him to be obedient with what he had around him.

Read Matthew 13:12 and Luke 16:10 and answer the following questions.

> *For whoever has, to him more shall be given, and he will have an abundance; but whoever does not have, even what he has shall be taken away from him.*
> **Matthew 13:12**

> *He who is faithful in a very little thing is faithful also in much; and he who is unrighteous in a very little thing is unrighteous also in much.*
> **Luke 16:10**

Restate Jesus' teaching in those two verses in your own words.

Why is it important to demonstrate faithfulness with what you have?

What are some reasons we might not be willing to use what God has given us?

Why might a person wait on God to give him more or to open doors rather than moving forward with what he has right now, in order to serve Him?

Describe the end result of not investing your spiritual gifts in those around you. How does this contribute to the continuation of a chaotic culture?

Faithfulness with what you have right now and right where you are is always the first step toward further use in God's kingdom. We see this not only with Gideon, but throughout the Bible, and in our own lives. We expect God to move in our lives, but we refuse to get going. Instead we stand still in place, waiting for the right time when all along God has given us everything we need. .

God wants you to follow Him right where you are. He wants you to be faithful now—whether it's with your family and friends or even in your neighborhood and church. Don't waste your time on visions of grandeur if you are not willing to get moving where God has placed you. Waiting on "the right time" can be an idol just like anything else.

List some of the benefits you receive when you choose to relinquish your plans and trust solely in God and His plan.

Despite having all of these benefits, why do you think some men still choose to "play it safe" and not risk full surrender to God's will and ways?

What might it look like for you to overcome the idol of comfort?

We experience our greatest spiritual success when we are willing to lay down our plans, purposes, devices, and strategies, and completely devote ourselves to God and His way. God is not interested in divided hearts. He wants your undivided attention, devotion, and obedience. He wants you to get up and get going toward the destiny He has created you to live out.

> The Lord has said, "For I know the plans that I have for you,' declares the LORD,
> 'plans for welfare and not for calamity to give you a future and a hope."
> **Jeremiah 29:11**

Life is not found in sitting around and waiting on the right time. Neither is it found in looking for other people to stand up and make a difference. You are to use your voice, your actions, and your life to advance God's kingdom agenda on earth. If, and when, enough kingdom men choose to rise up for what is right and just in this world, the enemy will be forced to back down. But we can only rise up when we are first willing to relinquish the plans and the idols who have locked us in place for far too long. God has given us all we need to get going. We need to take the steps He has laid before us.

Spend some time considering God's leading in your life to make a difference in your home, community and country. What do you believe God is asking you to do in order advance His kingdom of love, righteousness and justice on earth?

God will often use our skills and knowledge from past experiences in order to enable us to make a greater impact for good in the lives of those around us.

What are some identifiable skills and talents God has developed in you which could be used to further His plans for well-being in your circles of influence?

What will you do as a result of identifying these skills and talents and their potential impact for good?

What step you can take this week to break out of your comfort zone and seek to make a difference for God in an area you have never sought to before?

Pray about how you can rise up as a kingdom man in order to impact your home, church, community, country, and world. Ask God to reveal to you anything He has already equipped you with which can be used to bring about a positive impact on the lives of those around you. Ask Him for the wisdom and courage to go after the destiny and purpose He has for you to fulfill.

BIBLE STUDY 2
STAND IN THE GAP

Quick question for you, but relevant. Do you know that you are somebody special? You're not ordinary; you are extraordinary. You're not average; you're superlative. And because of this truth, God is calling you to do something bigger than you ever dreamed was possible.

But He needs to get you to get out of your wine press, like Gideon, and stop letting the culture hold you hostage. He needs you to deal with the idols that are consuming you, as well as those that surround you. He needs you to publicly and unashamedly decide, "Yes, I'm going to be defined by God now. And I'm going to let it be known that I don't deal with idols. I surrender to and follow the true and living God."

Read Ezekiel 22:30 then answer the following questions.

I searched for a man among them who would build up the wall and stand in the gap before Me for the land, so that I would not destroy it; but I found no one.
Ezekiel 22:30

How can a man "stand in the gap" before God?

What are some demonstrable actions a man can take to stand up for righteousness and justice in order to advance God's kingdom agenda?

God can give you the ability to stand up for Him. But it will take courage. Gideon was so frightened by the time God reached out to him that he was literally threshing wheat in a wine press. He was hiding so that the enemy would not see what he was doing and steal it. Yet by the end of the story of Gideon's life, he had risen to become a feared and honored man of great courage. In fact, he had so much courage that his reputation spread (Judg. 6:32).

You have all you need within you to do and be the same. But it will take standing up for what you believe in and following God's leading in your life. You can't remain hidden, seeking to protect what is yours, and expect to defeat the enemy. You have a choice to make. Will you live as a man of fear and preservation or will you lead those within your sphere of influence to spiritual victory as a kingdom man of courage?

What's the difference between "privately declaring" and "publicly proclaiming" your allegiance to God and standing for Him?

Why do you think so few men are willing to rise up and publicly align themselves with God in today's culture?

What are some strategies the enemy uses to keep a man silent on what is right and true?

Many men, like Gideon, are initially afraid to stand in the gap. Don't wait for absence of fear in order to step out in faith. Obedience as a kingdom man isn't always couched in calm. Sometimes that obedience takes place in a mixture of emotions. There is no doubt that Gideon was scared if he was traipsing around at night when he went to pull down his family's altars (Judg. 6:27).

Courage does not require the absence of fear. Courage means right actions taken in spite of fear's presence. There's nothing courageous about doing something you know will succeed without any opposition. Courage occurs when you rise up to do the task that looks impossible.

If we commit to "get going," how can our action steps override our fear?

Describe how Satan uses "fear" to paralyze people from doing what is right.

When has God helped you or someone you know push past your fears to make an impact? What did you learn from that experience?

Kingdom men exist today in the midst of a pagan nation, on many levels, numbed and held captive by fear. We are living in our own sort of Midian. We are sorely outnumbered. Our broader culture has not only abandoned God, but it has taken up the offensive against the one true God. Much of what our society values stands against key doctrines and beliefs from Scripture. This is our reality whether we like it or not. We can pretend it doesn't exist, but it does.

But it doesn't take millions to take ground back for Christ. In fact, as we saw in the story of Gideon, three hundred will do (see Judg. 7). Gideon demonstrated this truth as he led his charge in the dark night. Similarly, we are to rise up and get going to do what God has called each of us to do so that we might advance His kingdom agenda on earth. All we have to do is to get going and trust that God is on our side.

We must do this personally, and we must also do this collectively. If we sit around waiting for a majority, we will have waited too long. God knows how to handle the issues we face. It's our role to repent of our sins, clean up our own homes, trust God, and then do what He says. A few kingdom men in the hands of one mighty God can route any evil that opposes them.

Can you identify ways you may have been able to advance God's kingdom through something you said or did, but you chose not to out of fear?

What are some common fears that keep you from moving? List them below.

Looking at your fears, how might God be able to supply all you need despite your fears?

Where is God calling you to stand in the gap?

What is one step you can take this week to stand for God in this gap?

Thinking back over the two personal bible studies from this session, identify one area of growth and one action point.

Pray right now and commit your life to living courageously as a kingdom man. Ask God to make it clear to you the level of impact you are to have for His kingdom, His glory, and others' good. Also ask God as you pray that He will place men in your life whom you can disciple and lead so that more kingdom men can rise up to tackle the troubles suffocating us in our homes, churches, communities, and in our country.

By this all men will know that you are
My disciples, if you have love for one another.

JOHN 13:15

WEEK 5
GET ALONG

START

Share one key takeaway from last session's group or personal studies.

Last week we talked about how idols keep us stuck in place and stagnant in God's kingdom. This week we will tackle barriers that keep us from working together for our shared kingdom agenda.

What would happen if the players on a football team tried to run different plays at the same time? Why is unity essential for a team?

Why is maintaining unity of approach and purpose critical for life in the body of Christ?

True unity does not mean sameness. It does not mean we are to all like the same things, listen to the same music, talk the same way, or eat the same food. True unity is about something much bigger. Unity is about oneness of purpose. There is no better way I know to describe what true unity looks like other than sports. Anytime a sports team, in any sport, is not unified on a shared goal, they will suffer as a result. *Unity matters.*

While we realize this intrinsically about athletic competitions, we seem to forget that the same principle applies to kingdom disciples following Christ. Much of the chaos and defeat we are experiencing today is a result of illegitimate division in the church. Because we have failed to unify under the goal of advancing God's kingdom agenda on earth. The division in our culture, and in our church, racially, politically, and socially needs a group of kingdom men who will rise to dispel it while insisting on unity through all we say and do.

Ask someone to pray before watching the video teaching.

WATCH

Use this space to take notes during the video teaching.

MAN UP

Use the following questions to discuss the video teaching.

Read John 13:35 and John 17:20-21 together.

By this all men will know that you are My disciples, if you have love for one another.
John 13:35

I do not ask on behalf of these alone, but for those also who believe in Me through their word; that they may all be one; even as You, Father, are in Me and I in You, that they also may be in Us, so that the world may believe that You sent Me.
John 17:20-21

Why do you think demonstrating "love for one another" reveals to onlookers that we are Christ's kingdom disciples?

Christ prayed the verses in John 17 right before He was arrested and put on trial. Why would this have been so important to Jesus in His final earthly moments?

In a world of chaos and confusion, of disconnectedness and disunity, we're needing kingdom men to rise up and bring harmony where there's conflict, and peace where there is chaos. Now is the time to get along. God's men bear a unique responsibility to set the stage for a comeback and a healing in our lives and in our land. One of the things we must begin to grasp at a greater level is that God is a God of unity and togetherness. God does not hang out in atmospheres of division. He cannot. It goes against the nature of His being and essence.

Describe some ways men can "rise up and bring harmony" in the area of division and disunity in our land.

Ephesians 4:3 urges Christians to be "diligent to preserve the unity of the Spirit in the bond of peace." What does it means to "preserve" unity as opposed to "create" it?

Why do you think it is our role as believers to "preserve" unity?

Whose role is it to originate or create the unity we are to preserve?

In cooking and baking, eggs often act as an emulsifier—an ingredient that brings two other ingredients together. God has called His people to become the emulsifiers in the culture. We have the opportunity to set the temperature on issues like racial relationships, family life, and increasing political division. We do this based on God's standard, not based on how we were raised, the color of our skin, or the class that we are. Before and beyond all those designations, we are primarily men of God.

What are some of the challenges we may face, or have faced, in seeking to unify relationships across racial, social, or political divides?

God has a standard. It's a high standard that involves living in love and unity. He is calling each of us—as much as it depends on us—to live at peace with everyone (Rom. 12:18). Unity requires intentional effort and calls us out of our comfort zone. But God never said that living as a kingdom man was easy. Nothing worthwhile comes easy. But it will be worth it as we impact our broken and chaotic culture with the healing balm of oneness.

Share one practical action you can put in place this week to intentionally preserve unity where disunity has taken hold. Make it personal It could be something you do at work, home, on social media, or in your church and community.

PRAYER

Father, in a culture that consistently promotes disunity, division, distrust, anger and blame—help us to be kingdom men who honor and reflect You through all we say and do. Grant us the wisdom and courage necessary to stand strong as men of unity in a world of hate. Bring unity where there is division and help us to be men of peace who accomplish much for your kingdom. In Christ's name, amen.

IDENTIFYING YOUR IDENTITY

We didn't get to experience the 2020 Olympics due to the difficulties in our world at the time. But if you have seen the Olympics at any other point in history, you know that one thing remains the same. When an athlete wins a competition, they do not ask the athlete what his or her favorite song is, and then play it. No, the song that plays when an athlete wins a competition is the song of the nation he or she represents. This is because his or her identity with their nation supersedes all else at that point in time.

Unfortunately, far too many Christians allow anything and everything to define them these days rather than the One who died for them, and lives in them: Jesus Christ. Because of this, we have identity confusion breeding illegitimate division everywhere. My favorite verse in the Bible, and a great verse on unity, is Galatians 2:20.

Read this verse and examine the following principles taken from it:

I have been crucified with Christ; and it is no longer I who live, but Christ lives in me; and the life which I now live in the flesh I live by faith in the Son of God, who loved me and gave Himself up for me.
Galatians 2:20

1 DEFINE YOUR HUMANITY BY YOUR CHRISTIANITY.

In English, the job of the adjective is to modify the noun. The adjective describes the noun. As a kingdom man, Christian is to be the adjective which defines you. Not your race, creed, culture, background, perspectives, or preferences. Whenever these things conflict with the living God as the modifier of who you are, you must adjust and align yourself once again under Him.

2 LAY DOWN YOUR OWN DESIRES.

Make God's standards and His rules your overarching desires. When Paul writes that "it is no longer I who live," he is stating that Christ now lives in him. Similarly, Christ now lives in each of us. We are His servants and we are to honor Him by living according to His desires, not our own.

3 LIVE BY FAITH IN THE SON OF GOD.

Find friends who will hold you accountable to living a life of faith according to Christ's standards and His rule of love. Take time to assess your relationships and if there is consistent disunity in any of them, seek to address it. Surround yourself with like-minded individuals who will also seek to preserve the unity of the Spirit in the bond of Christ.

Which of these principles do you need to take hold of most today?
Spend a few minutes praying to God.

BIBLE STUDY 1
GOD DID IT

When things go wrong in your life, where do you look first? Do you try and find how you may have contributed to what went wrong or are you quick to blame someone or something else?

Oftentimes it feels easier to blame something outside of ourselves when we go through troubles in life. But there is someone we rarely think to blame, who may actually be behind the issues we are facing. God Himself. To be clear, God is never responsible for evil or suffering. He cannot sin or cause sin, it is against His holy nature. However, God will often allow us to sit in the disorder of our lives in order that we might return to Him and experience refreshing and revival.

God doesn't stir up issues for us to deal with just for the fun of it. But He does allow negative consequences in our lives to crop up when He is trying to get our attention. Rather than pointing fingers at everyone else when difficulties arise, we might want to take a moment to focus on the One who is really in charge. When we do, we will find that the way to solve life's challenging situations is sometimes easier than we had once thought.

In the history of Israel and Judah, Asa was one of the better kings, particularly during the first part of his reign. In 2 Chronicles 15, the Spirit of God came upon the prophet Azariah to encourage Asa in his religious reforms and remind him what happens when people forsake God.

Read 2 Chronicles 15:3-6 and answer the following questions.

For many days Israel was without the true God and without a teaching priest and without law. But in their distress they turned to the LORD God of Israel, and they sought Him, and He let them find Him. In those times there was no peace to him who went out or to him who came in, for many disturbances afflicted all the inhabitants of the lands. Nation was crushed by nation, and city by city, for God troubled them with every kind of distress. But you, be strong and do not lose courage, for there is reward for your work.

2 Chronicles 15:3-6

Why would God trouble the Israelites "with every kind of distress?"

Do you believe that God still does that toward groups of people, congregations or nations today? Can you think of any examples that you feel may be from God's hand?

Can you identify a time in your life when you can see God allowed troubles in order to draw you back to Him and His rule over you?

Like the Israelites, in what ways does our distress have a way of making us turn back to God?

During the season that I wrote this Bible study and the book that goes with it, we as a nation and the world were in the middle of multiple simultaneous pandemics. We were facing dual pandemics: a medical pandemic and a cultural pandemic. Yet, deeper still and at the root of both of these sat a spiritual pandemic.

What I noticed as I observed all that took place during the onset of this unusual time, is that we had wandered far from the value system established by God for how human beings are to live, act, and relate to one another. What's more—our wandering had gone on for far too long. Across racial and class lines we had come up with our own standards for how we should treat each other, and it had not done us any good.

As we saw in the passage we just read, God will occasionally allow unrest in order to urge His people to a heartfelt call on Him for help. He has to let His people hit rock bottom in order that we might discover He truly is the Rock at the bottom. Sometimes it takes a mess to make a miracle.

What are some ways God purges us as individuals, as well as collectively in the body of Christ, of sinful toxins permeating this world?

List three sins or cultural problems that need to be purged from our culture today, in order to be replaced by God's rule:

1. _____

2. _____

3. _____

What can be done in order to help remove these problems and replace them with the truth of God's Word and healing power of His love?

Problems abound in our culture today. We certainly have plenty for God to say, "Enough is enough!" But if we miss the reality that God has allowed disorder in order to bring about a correction and a cleaning, then we will just move from one symptom to another symptom. We will miss the opportunity to address the root that has produced the fruit that has led to the confusion of hopelessness on display.

The root of the problems we face in our churches, culture, and country today are clearly spiritual. To repair and restore our culture we must understand the spiritual components behind our problems before proposing pragmatic solutions to these crises.

To briefly examine one problem among many, over the past several years our national conversation has returned again and again to race and racism. Racism isn't a bad habit. It isn't a mistake. It is sin. The answer is not sociology, it's theology. Kingdom men need to be just as bold in speaking out against the sin of racism as other sins when they confront it in others. Kingdom men must also be willing to examine their own hearts for areas of racism, resentment, anger, and division.

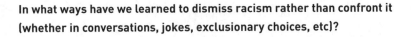

In what ways have we learned to dismiss racism rather than confront it (whether in conversations, jokes, exclusionary choices, etc)?

List some practical things that can be done in order to be proactive about ridding our culture from racism?

Do you think God wants us to be proactive about ridding our culture of racism? Why or why not?

In addition to racism, what other cultural problems do we need to take a spiritual driven approach to resolving? List the problem and a few steps to resolve them.

Pray about your personal perspective on racism, and the division of the races or ethnicities in our nation. Ask God to reveal to you any areas where you may hold prejudice or pride in your heart, and then ask His forgiveness if He does reveal any. Take a moment to think about the purpose and power of unity and then ask the Spirit to show you how you can be more intentional about combating and overturning disunity in your spheres of influence.

BIBLE STUDY 2
THE GOSPEL AND RACE

When the subject of race relations came to a boiling point in our culture in the midst of 2020, I heard from a number of my white friends concerning both their confusion and personal conviction. While none of them considered themselves racist, there was new insight into what it meant to oppose racism. It didn't involve merely not being racist yourself. Rather, this time the conversation included topics of what people were willing to do in order to combat racism in our society at large.

There are two types of sin in Scripture. But most of us examine our actions based on only one type. When we do that, we fail to take account of our whole experience and become less able to deal with the root issues.

The first type of sin is called sins of commission. This is when you or I do something that is inherently wrong. I won't go into a lot of details on this because most of us are aware of what this is. But there is another type of sin which goes largely ignored. It's called the sin of omission.

Read James 4:17 and answer the following questions.

Therefore, to one who knows the right thing to do and does not do it, to him it is sin.

James 4:17

On a scale of 1-10, how aware were you of this type of sin (omission)?

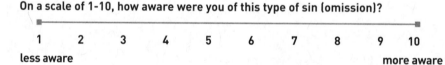

1	2	3	4	5	6	7	8	9	10

less aware   more aware

Why do you think there is less emphasis on the sin found in James 4:17 by spiritual leaders than other, more actively apparent sins?

In your experience, how aware are most people about sins of omission? Why are these sins easier to ignore?

Read Micah 6:8 and circle what the prophet Micah wrote the Lord calls us to do.

He has told you, O man, what is good;
And what does the LORD require of you
But to do justice, to love kindness,
And to walk humbly with your God?
Micah 6:8

How does failing to do what the Lord requires here a sin of omission?
List a few examples.

Most of us know the right things to do. Sin here isn't a knowledge problem, but an action problem. To use racism as an example, when someone says to me, "I'm not racist," I am glad to hear they feel that way and I do hope it's true. But Micah 6:8 isn't about "not doing injustice." It isn't about not being a racist, either, to put it in context with our contemporary conversation.

Micah 6:8 doesn't call us to "love justice." Neither does it call us to "affirm justice." This passage specifically calls us to *do* justice. In Hebrew, this word could be translated "make" or "manufacture." God is asking us to take action.

According to the Word of God, we are to actively "do justice." What are some ways we can actively "do justice?"

What tangible step can you take this week to "do justice?"

How is doing justice, related to loving mercy and walking humbly with God?

God has spoken on the issues at hand, and He has not stuttered. He has spoken about racism. He has spoken about systemic and individual injustices. He has spoken about classism. He has spoken about culturalism. He has spoken about equity, elitism, empathy, and more. Just read the Book of James. That's a great place to start to learn. God has spoken about all of these subjects, but until we align our hearts, thoughts, words, and actions underneath His overarching rule, we are living in sin.

Righteousness and justice can be defined in the following ways:

- Righteousness is the moral standard of right and wrong to which God holds people accountable based on His divine standard.
- Justice is the equitable and impartial application of God's moral law in society.

> *Righteousness and justice are the foundation of Your throne;*
> *Lovingkindness and truth go before You.*
> Psalm 89:14

Based on those definitions and these words from the psalmist, answer the following questions.

Why is it important to balance both righteousness and justice?

Do you naturally give more attention to one or the other? Explain.

Can you name a contemporary example of pursuing righteousness and justice simultaneously?

Who are some role models for you who have lived committed to both righteousness and justice?

God desires that we live our lives embracing both righteousness and justice. We are to do what is right but we are also to stand up and speak out for others in need. These actions promote an atmosphere of justice for everyone. Far too often, we confuse "justice" as that which gives someone who has done wrong what he or she deserves. But when God refers to "justice" in this particular passage, He is speaking about ensuring that all people are treated fairly and equitably.

When men decide to stand together for what is right and just in society, we can make a difference. We can change the trajectory of our culture. We can influence others for good by advancing God's kingdom agenda on earth. We do this primarily through the spread of the gospel.

Unity isn't just about getting along; it's about getting things done. We'll never experience a movement of kingdom men rising in our nation until we have kingdom men relating to each other in the body of Christ in an authentic, mutually honoring manner. Racial reconciliation isn't about playing a video of an ethnic preacher to your white church on Sunday, or vice versa, reading books on racism, or posing online. While those things are good, they—in and of themselves—are not unity. Unity takes place when people join together with oneness of purpose. It is working together in harmony toward a shared vision and goal. Unity involves doing justice together, not just talking about it.

Pray for open doors to share the gospel with others. Also take time to ask God for ways that you can be more proactive in "doing justice" within your spheres of influence. Pray for your small group and ask for insight from the Holy Spirit on ways your small group can tear down the walls of racism in order to advance the love of God through the gospel of Christ to a world in need.

Then Joshua said to the people,
"Consecrate yourselves, for tomorrow
the LORD will do wonders among you."

JOSHUA 3:5

WEEK 6
SETTING
THE STAGE

START

Welcome to group session 6 of *Kingdom Men Rising.*

Last week we talked about the call for kingdom men to get along. In the personal studies we looked at the crucial aspect of race and racism.

What was one lesson you learned from Dr. Evans' teaching on race?

This week we will be we be talking about the crucial spiritual disciplines for kingdom men.

Share a time when you have had to trust God, though your circumstances were overwhelming.

During the year this study was written (2020), the world was turned completely upside down. From global pandemic caused by a virus infecting millions to the economic repercussions that followed, to the cultural unrest wrought by racial tensions, the year was daunting for many of us. Yet, despite all our hardships, time will tell and begin to reveal the faithfulness of God throughout a troubling year. Perhaps you're seeing the fruit of His faithfulness despite overwhelming circumstances. Often, God uses our circumstances to set the stage for His incredible faithfulness.

Today, we'll look at an event in the life of Israel where God asked His people to show up. He was setting the stage for them to take their place in the land that He had promised. All they needed to do was show up, prepare themselves, and follow God's directions.

Ask someone to pray before watching the video teaching.

Setting the Stage
WATCH

Use this space to take notes during the video teaching.

MAN UP

Use the following questions to discuss the video teaching.

Read Joshua 3:5 together.

*Then Joshua said to the people, "Consecrate yourselves,
for tomorrow the LORD will do wonders among you."*
Joshua 3:5

Prior to Joshua leading the Israelites across the Jordan River and into the promised land, God asked him and the people to do something. He asked them to "consecrate" themselves. To "consecrate" means to dedicate something or someone to a special purpose or service.

God asked that Joshua and the people of Israel dedicate themselves for one purpose—crossing the Jordan River. He asked them to focus. He asked them to prepare themselves—emotionally, spiritually and physically—for what He was about to do for them and through them.

> **What might it look like for us to "consecrate" ourselves or set ourselves apart for God's purposes today?**

> **How does God grow us as we prepare to serve Him?**

The people of Israel would have to trust God to make it across the Jordan. That's why their preparation mattered. Israel was to set out across the Jordan River at the height of flood season. The water spilled over the banks, and the ground beneath the waters was muddy. God would need to perform two miracles in getting the Israelites across the pregnant river. He would need to stop the waters from flowing but He would also need to dry up the land enough for them to cross.

> **Imagine standing on the shores of the river knowing that somehow the next day you and thousands of people, animals, carts and belongings would somehow need to cross. What do you think the Israelites were thinking the day before they were to cross the Jordan River? What reasons did they have to be confident in God?**

Life gets overwhelming, sometimes. We get overwhelmed with medical disasters, career challenges, financial burdens and troubles with our family or culture. We live in a flood zone, and often the flood is overwhelming, but as Dr. Evans said during flood season, God is setting the stage for the supernatural to invade the natural to show us how big God really is. God allows flood season so that He can demonstrate He alone is God.

How has God demonstrated to you that He alone is God, during a difficult time in your life?

Only God could have performed the miracles necessary to get thousands across the Jordan River. He worked that way so that all the credit would be His. To remember what God had done, the Israelites took twelve stones from the Jordan and placed them in their camp. All throughout the Scriptures God calls His people to remember what He's done and share His work with others.

How can we use the opportunities we have to witness God's strength and power in our lives?

How can we create a culture where men feel a greater need to focus on God and consecrate themselves for the purpose of witnessing God's greater involvement in their circumstances?

Who needs to hear about how God has been faithful to you through a flood season? When will you set aside time to tell them?

PRAYER

Father, You have the power not only to dry up the flood waters which seek to overwhelm us but You can also help us pass through the storm on the firmness of dry land. Help us to keep our eyes on You, stay focused on You, and consecrate ourselves to do the work of Your kingdom. In Christ's name, amen.

THREE PRINCIPLES FOR A PURPOSE-FILLED LIFE

Never measure God's movement without first taking a look at your own. Far too often, God is waiting on us as men to do something before He will make His move. Whether it is Moses holding out the rod before He parts the sea, or Peter keeping his eyes on Jesus before He rescues him from the storm—God frequently waits to see how we respond in faith before He fully reveals His hand in our lives.

In the story we are studying this week found in Joshua 3:7-17, the priests had to literally "walk by faith" before they would see God move. They had to put their feet in the water prior to God parting it for all to cross. Their example reveals three important principles we should all live by as kingdom men: Listen, Obey, and Stand.

LISTEN

The priests had been asked to dedicate themselves for the specific task at hand—stepping into the flooding Jordan River. In order to do this, they needed to focus on what God said by consecrating themselves before Him. They wouldn't be able to hear Him if they had distractions in their lives at that time. Kingdom men need to set aside distractions in our lives as well so we can better hear God in order to understand His instructions clearly.

What are you hearing from God recently?

OBEY

I don't know about you, but stepping into the water of a river in order to get that same water to go away doesn't make a whole lot of sense to me. Yet that is what God asked the priests to do. Obeying God as a kingdom man doesn't always involve understanding His methods. Faith doesn't always make sense. But it can make miracles. Be willing to obey God when He makes your part in His plan clear to you.

Look back to the question on the last page. How are you obeying based on the time you spend listening to God?

STAND

In verse 17 we read that the priests had to stand their ground in order for the Israelites to pass safely. It says,

> *And the priests who carried the ark of the covenant of the LORD stood firm on dry ground in the middle of the Jordan while all Israel crossed on dry ground, until all the nation had finished crossing the Jordan.*

Kingdom men must never waiver when called upon to serve God. Standing in the middle of what was previously a raging river isn't the safest place to be, from a human perspective, but God doesn't call us to live safely, He calls us to live by faith. Sometimes that means standing strong where you are and in what you believe in so that those you love can get to where they need to go as well.

Why is it better to trust in God's power than in human limitations?

LIFE ON LIFE DISCIPLESHIP

Developing strong muscles involves a process of tearing the fibers in your body in order to give your body the opportunity to produce muscle growth. The process of building muscles is painful because you cannot strengthen your muscles any other way.

Similarly, developing your spiritual walk as a kingdom man often comes during the difficulties and painful scenarios of life. That is when most men will see the most growth, if we respond to our challenges rightly. Yet if you choose to simply nurse your wound and complain about the experience, you will not grow. It's only when you push through the pain that you discover glory on the other side.

Read Ephesians 1:11 and answer the following questions.

We have obtained an inheritance, having been predestined according to His purpose who works all things after the counsel of His will.
Ephesians 1:11

Summarize this verse in your own words.

In what ways can God use pain and brokenness "after the counsel of His will" (see Romans 8:28)?

What might it look like to develop your spiritual muscles? In what ways might that process be painful?

Why must we grow to in order to help others grow others?

Kingdom men have obtained a spiritual inheritance from the Lord, but this inheritance is not only for them, it is for all who come into contact with them. To honor what they've been given, kingdom men must focus on their spiritual growth and development. It is the responsibility of every kingdom man to take the kingdom inheritance and share it with others. This is the process of discipleship. It is the process where one kingdom man takes the values of the kingdom and transfers them to another who will then transfer them to another man.

This is our responsibility. This is what Abraham did with his son Isaac. What Elijah did with Elisha. What Jesus did with the Twelve. What Paul did with Timothy. We are to do nothing less. Even if that means stepping out of your comfort zone. Standing for God will not always be popular, but it will always reap rewards.

Why is it often easier to go with the flow of cultural norms rather than speak up for God's truth in the midst of worldliness?

When has following God called you to step out of your comfort zone? What did you learn?

Think of someone who impacted your own spiritual growth. Describe qualities about this person which stand out to you.

Discipleship takes boldness. Confidence. Love. Awareness. Commitment. Perhaps you used some of these traits to describe the person in the previous question. Difficult conversations on subjects of truth, sin, and redemption aren't easy. They require courage. People don't always want to hear the truth. Discipleship isn't necessarily fun. But neither are drills, conditioning, or weight lifting. Yet all of that is necessary to strengthen our muscles. Similarly, discipleship is necessary for a kingdom man to pass on a spiritual inheritance.

Transferring kingdom values must take place on a regular basis through personal examples and authentic conversations about those examples. It's not done only through seminars, books, or radio broadcasts. Those things are good, but they are supplemental.

The transferring of kingdom values, as clearly outlined in Scripture, takes place person to person and heart to heart, like Paul instructed his young kingdom protege, Timothy.

You therefore, my son, be strong in the grace that is in Christ Jesus. The things which you have heard from me in the presence of many witnesses, entrust these to faithful men who will be able to teach others also.
2 Timothy 2:1–2.

Define "discipleship" based on the Scriptures above.

In what ways does discipleship influence and impact our culture for good?

Who discipled you? Who can you disciple?

At the root of all the issues we face in our nation, communities, churches, families and in our own individual lives is this lack of transference of kingdom values. Discipleship is a simple process, but it isn't easy. That's why we need to be strong in the grace Jesus gives. However, we can always be certain, the grace we need will always be supplied as we become more like Jesus.

Read Luke 6:40 and John 13:15 and answer the following questions:

A pupil is not above his teacher; but everyone, after he has been fully trained, will be like his teacher.
Luke 6:40

For I (Jesus) gave you an example that you also should do as I did to you.
John 13:15

Describe the cycle of discipleship, based on these two verses.

Why is it sometimes tempting to leave the role of "discipleship" to those we consider to be "professional Christians" like pastors and small group leaders?

What should it teach us that Jesus' first disciples were ordinary men with no formal education?

Transferring kingdom principles doesn't only happen in small group settings when we share about past adventures, although that is important. Life lessons often must be experienced by the individuals themselves in order to root deeply. Discipleship doesn't take place only through discourse. It comes through relationship, partnering, and doing life together.

Yet it seems that we often get so focused on weekly meetings, or programs that we have forgotten this truth. We have forgotten what actually accomplishes the outcomes we desire and so desperately need. Especially when you are standing on a riverbank staring at a raging river you have been asked to cross with your family, livestock, and possessions.

The Israelites faced this river in Joshua chapter 3. But we as men face our own rivers today. In order to rise up and cross through that which seeks to stop us, we are going to need to commit to this thing called "doing life together." We are going to need to embrace the call to kingdom discipleship on a deeper level.

Pray about anything in your life that may inhibit you from fully living out your call to be discipled and disciple others. Ask God to remove any obstacles in your way so that you can leave an impact on the lives of those around you. Be willing to embrace life's difficulties and pain as a way of growing spiritually, and spend some time seeking the Spirit's discernment on how you are to grow through the challenges you face.

BIBLE STUDY 2
TAKE A STEP. GRAB A STONE.

Read Joshua 4:1-24 before completing this study.

It's fun to get to see God show up in your life. It is in those times when He makes Himself real that our faith grows and we discover the satisfying feeling that comes with resting in God. But like a Super Bowl winning team who becomes too content with their victory, reveling in the past won't do a whole lot for your future. What's more, it won't do anything for anyone else's future either.

What would happen to a championship sports team who decided to focus more on the previous year's championship than on the next season?

Have you ever noticed the slumps that can occur for business executives, athletes or any others after a momentous accomplishment is made? What would you say attributes to that slump?

How can you guard yourself from falling into a similar slump after spiritual victory or success?

The miracle of the crossing of the Jordan River was a tremendous miracle, on all fronts. But God didn't want the miracle to get lost in the merriment of its celebration. He knew that He needed to seed this miracle deep into the hearts and minds of the Israelites. He chose to do this by having them set up what we often call "stones of remembrance." These enormous stones would serve as a reminder to them about what God did to provide a way out when there was no way as He ushered them into the promised land.

But God didn't have Joshua set up just one place of stones. One set of stones would remain in the middle of the Jordan River (4:9). The other would be set up at Gilgal, the city where Israel established their first camp (4:20), and serve as a reminder as well as a conversation-starter for generations to come.

Why did God call Israel to set up stones in the middle of a river where no one would see them again?

Why does God ask us to continually remember what He has done for us?

"To this day" (v. 9) is a repeated phrase in Joshua. While we might not make monuments to God's faithfulness like the Israelites, what are some ways we can keep the work of the Lord in the front of our hearts and minds?

The stones placed in the river would be visible during the dry season as a reminder that at one time thousands crossed the dry river. The stones in the camp were a reminder to all who encamped at Gilgal. God did not want the Israelites to forget what He had done there for them. He didn't want them to forget where they came from and how they had gotten there. He had them set up a perpetual reminder that it was not by their might nor by their power that they had come this far. The twelve stones solemnly declared that they were there because of the supernatural hand of God.

"To this day" is a repeated phrase in the Book of Joshua. It is a signal for us to pause and remember the work of the Lord. God does this for the Israelites' good. He had seen how quickly His people had forgotten the miracle of the ten plagues, the parting of the Red Sea, the food in the barren desert, and the water from a rock. He knew His people were prone to forgetfulness. So this time, He established a visible reminder of His sovereignty in the midst of humanity's struggles.

Remembering who God is and what He has done is critical for each of us if we are to effectively transfer the principles of biblical manhood throughout the generations. That's one reason God emphasized this so much in Scripture.

Read the following verses and circle or underline any repeated concepts.

Only give heed to yourself and keep your soul diligently, so that you do not forget the things which your eyes have seen and they do not depart from your heart all the days of your life; but make them known to your sons and your grandsons.
Deuteronomy 4:9

Then it shall come about when the LORD your God brings you into the land which He swore to your fathers, Abraham, Isaac and Jacob, to give you, great and splendid cities which you did not build, and houses full of all good things which you did not fill, and hewn cisterns which you did not dig, vineyards and olive trees which you did not plant, and you eat and are satisfied, then watch yourself, that you do not forget the LORD who brought you from the land of Egypt, out of the house of slavery.
Deuteronomy 6:10–12

Beware that you do not forget the LORD your God by not keeping His commandments and His ordinances and His statutes which I am commanding you today.
Deuteronomy 8:11

Then your heart will become proud and you will forget the LORD your God who brought you out from the land of Egypt, out of the house of slavery.
Deuteronomy 8:14

But you shall remember the LORD your God, for it is He who is giving you power to make wealth, that He may confirm His covenant which He swore to your fathers, as it is this day. It shall come about if you ever forget the LORD your God and go after other gods and serve them and worship them, I testify against you today that you will surely perish. Like the nations that the LORD makes to perish before you, so you shall perish; because you would not listen to the voice of the LORD your God.
Deuteronomy 8:18–20

What are some of the recurring themes that show up in these passages?

What are some common outcomes which happen when we do "forget" God?

What processes do you have in place to remember what God has done?

How has God set the stage for your spiritual success lately?

How are these memories helpful to you as you seek to disciple other men?

God does miraculous work in His people's lives all of the time. But the problems arise when we forget what He has done and, as a result, either start taking the credit for ourselves or ignore His future guidance, or both. Setting up reminders of what God has done and how He has worked not only serves a mechanism for our own personal spiritual stability and growth, but it also enables us to become better at sharing about the details of His power with others.

Take some time to think through ways you might want to memorialize events in your life where God has worked wonders. Pray and ask for the Spirit's guidance as you look to keep the memories of these breakthroughs fresh somehow. Also seek God's hand and will for how you can better share about these testimonies in your life so that other people may become challenged to grow in their faith as well.

A good man leaves an inheritance
to his children's children,
And the wealth of the sinner
is stored up for the righteous.

PROVERBS 13:22

FURTHERING THE FUTURE

START

Last session, we talked about how God sets the stage for our greatest spiritual victories and how He expects us to pass those blessings on through the process of discipleship.

Based on your personal study last week, what does it mean to "pass the baton" spiritually?

What would happen to a professional relay-race team if they kept dropping the baton? What would be an example of spiritually dropping the baton?

No matter how quickly you run in a relay, you will lose if you do not pass the baton. We've all seen a relay race team pull out in front only to come to a screeching halt when the baton drops. Determination quickly changes into despair and frustration. The baton drops; the race is over.

While we understand this principle when it comes to running relay races, we have somehow failed to grasp its importance when it comes to living as kingdom men. Part of being a kingdom man is the successful passing of the baton. The buck doesn't stop with you. Nor do God's kingdom values. We desperately need more men to realize this and rise up to fulfill this great purpose in the body of Christ today.

Ask someone to pray before watching the video teaching.

Furthering the Future

WATCH

Use this space to take notes during the video teaching.

MAN UP

Read Proverbs 13:22 together.

A good man leaves an inheritance to his children's children,
And the wealth of the sinner is stored up for the righteous.
Proverbs 13:22

Kingdom men pass on a spiritual inheritance to those who come behind them. While Proverbs refers to one's direct descendants, the spiritual principle transcends your immediate family. Anyone who is within your spheres of influence ought to have a greater awareness of God and His kingdom values because of their relationship with you. Each man pursues that goal differently, but we all share the same goal—transferring kingdom values to future generations.

To pass on kingdom values we have to be generationally minded and not merely personally fulfilled." Describe the differences between being "generationally minded" as opposed to "personally fulfilled."

Describe a time when you witnessed the successful transfer of kingdom values (whether to you from someone else, or from you to someone else).

What happens if we don't make transferring kingdom values a priority?

Fatherhood is misunderstood in our culture. Fatherlessness has reached epidemic proportions. Even among stable homes, a father may say he needs to "babysit" his own kids while his wife goes out. However, fathers don't babysit; they parent. Too many fathers allow teaching and discipleship to fall to someone else.

Why do you suppose so many men are sitting on the sidelines of their families?

Read Deuteronomy 6:7 and answer the following questions.

You shall teach them diligently to your sons and shall talk of
them when you sit in your house and when you walk by the
way and when you lie down and when you rise up.

Deuteronomy 6:7

To whom is this verse directed? What does this teach about a father's involvement in his children's life?

How might this verse apply to those of us without children? How might a man with no physical descendants impact the next generation?

We often hear a lot of complaints about the next generation. But those complaints tend to arise out of armchair-quarterback fathers. If and when fathers fail to lead by example, investing in the lives of their children and also in those within their spheres of influence, it only makes sense that there is a breakdown in the culture. We are all part of the process of impacting each other as iron sharpens iron in order to develop each other for kingdom success.

Small steps of discipleship lead to larger steps of discipleship, whether it is with your own children or with those in your spheres of influence.

Identify ways that each of you in the small group can add small, yet intentional, steps of discipleship to your normal routine. Seek to implement these small steps and then discuss how it went when you get together next time.

PRAYER

Father, in a world full of selfishness, You ask us to think of others by investing in them through an intentional pursuit of spiritual training. Enable us to identify those within our spheres of influence who we can impact for Your kingdom and the greater good of all involved. Open doors for us to have significant influence on those we know and love. In Christ's name, amen.

FAMILY, FAITH, AND FAVOR

God has given us three distinct things to pass down as kingdom men to the next generation. These three things are found in the blessing of the covenant. Passing these down won't happen just because you want it to happen. It will require your intentional engagement and pursuit. They are: Family, Faith, and Favor.

FAMILY

Kingdom men need to be men who embrace family on every level. We need to be like a city set on a hill, displaying the light that comes from a fully functioning family. Whether that means modeling and mentoring on the role of father, son, brother, cousin, uncle, or grandson—family roles should be taken seriously and honored. We do this by living authentically within each role, being responsible for what needs to be done. We also do this by discipling others in our family as they live out their various roles.

FAITH

Kingdom men are men of faith. To be a man of faith means that you allow your decisions to come underneath the rule of God in every area of your life. We sometimes confuse acting on faith to include a trek off the beaten path. But often it is the man who offers consistency and stability for his loved ones and who exhibits the greatest faith. Faith involves placing God's will for your life above your own will and desires. When you do that, you will not only demonstrate what a kingdom man of faith looks like, but you will also be investing in the faith of those who look to you for guidance as well.

FAVOR

Kingdom men recognize the difference between personal gain and God's blessing. God's blessing comes from His hand, great peace is found within it. Proverbs puts it like this:

It is the blessing of the LORD that makes rich,
And He adds no sorrow to it.
PROVERBS 10:22

Divine favor is a key aspect of the blessing because God alone is able to supply all that a person needs. When you learn to rest in God's favor, you will also be positioned to teach others how to do the same. But as long as you are striving after your own personal success, apart from God's leading in your life, you will be dropping the baton of favor which is yours to pass to the next generation.

A kingdom man always majors on the majors: Family, Faith and Favor. When these three things are flowing according to God's plan for your life, you will impact future generations for Christ.

How are you thankful for the family, faith, and favor God has given you?

How are you passing them down to the next generation?

BIBLE STUDY 1
A LEGACY OF LOVE

You've likely seen the word "legacy" attached to sports, athletes, business owners, employees, volunteers, mentors, coaches, friends, and more, because it's all about passing down the DNA of greatness. These principles apply to all of us in the body of Christ too. Legacy involves your impact on others. It's the spiritual DNA you pass down.

The question each of us must ask is: What kind of legacy am I leaving?

Read Genesis 1:28 and answer the following questions.

> *God blessed them; and God said to them, "Be fruitful and multiply, and fill the earth, and subdue it; and rule over the fish of the sea and over the birds of the sky and over every living thing that moves on the earth."*
> **Genesis 1:28**

This verse is God's commission to Adam and Eve. Restate this command in your own words.

How might Adam have obeyed this commandment in the garden of Eden?

How might we obey it in the places where God has placed us?

How would our homes, workplaces, churches and communities look differently if more men lived this direction for the Lord out today?

Every human being is an image-bearer. Being made in God's image means that every person is like God in ways that other created beings are not. We have souls, and the capacity for reason and relationships. We are creative and industrious, like God.

Adam left the garden, but every kingdom has the same commission as Adam—to fill the world with people who know and love God. To be about the work of passing on the spiritual inheritance of a comprehensive theistic world view.

Two predominant grids operate on this earth: humanism and theism. Humanism focuses what mankind wants, thinks, and determines. Functioning according to humanism is like putting on sunglasses filtered to reveal the ego's world view. Conversely, theism filters everything through the lens of God's divine perspective.

As kingdom men, we are created and called to transfer a theistic viewpoint to those within our spheres of influence. In this way, we pass on the DNA of the covenant infused in the creation mandate found in Genesis 1:28.

What are the differences between humanism and theism?

In what ways does humanism bleed into our Christian culture?

Why do you think so many men consider humanism an acceptable grid by which to function?

Adam wasn't commissioned to fill the earth with an accumulation of accolades, achievements, and material wealth. God called Adam to fill the earth with His image. A divine inheritance isn't about houses, clothes, cars, fame, or money. Divine inheritances start with the transfer of the faith. It doesn't matter how much money a man has if he does not have the foundation of a solid faith. Without biblical values, it will all come crashing down when the storms of life roll in.

How do biblical values and a solid faith help a person, family or community during difficulties in life?

What are some of the common difficulties we are facing as men in our culture?

In what ways can we seek to infuse biblical values into the solution steps of these issues?

Many of us know we ought to live passionate for God's kingdom but aren't clear on what that means. Thankfully, when Christ came to fulfill the commandments, He gave us one summary commandment in place of all of them. This is what it means to follow God. Furthering the future means obeying this command and training others to do likewise.

> One of them, a lawyer, asked Him a question, testing Him, "Teacher, which is the great commandment in the Law?" And He said to him, "'YOU SHALL LOVE THE LORD YOUR GOD WITH ALL YOUR HEART, AND WITH ALL YOUR SOUL, AND WIT ALL YOUR MIND.' This is the great and foremost commandment. The second is like it, 'YOU SHALL LOVE YOUR NEIGHBOR AS YOURSELF.' On these two commandments depend the whole Law and the Prophets."
> **Matthew 22:35-40**

Jesus told us that if and when we choose to love, we are fulfilling the commandments. Love is compassionately and righteously pursuing the well-being of another. Thankfully, Scripture helps us out here as well. Consider this biblical definition of love.

> Love is patient, love is kind and is not jealous; love does not brag and is not arrogant, does not act unbecomingly; it does not seek its own, is not provoked, does not take into account a wrong suffered, does not rejoice in unrighteousness, but rejoices with the truth; bears all things, believes all things, hopes all things, endures all things.
> **1 Corinthians 13:4-7**

Far too often we relegate 1 Corinthians 13:4-7, a passage which describes love, as a wedding section of the Bible. While these verses apply to marriages, they also apply to everything we are to do and be as kingdom men. Let's take a look at them, but this time through the lens of biblical manhood.

How would emphasizing love positively impact our homes, communities, churches, and society?

What thoughts or hurdles tempt you away from responding to life's difficulties or relational issues with love?

How can we as men make the qualities of love more prevalent in society?

The greatest men in the kingdom of God understand that love isn't only something we do on an anniversary or holiday. Love ought to be the way we roll, with everyone. Sometimes we may get hung up on the emotional aspects associated with the term that we fail to miss what love truly means. Love is a default posture of our heart and lives. It is who God is and who we ought to be.

What are some ways men might model the qualities of love found in 1 Corinthians 13?

How might you specifically model this type of love?

Pray and ask God to nurture and strengthen the nine listed qualities of love in your own life so that you are better prepared to disciple others on how to live out these qualities in their own lives. Spend some time searching Scriptures to better describe these qualities in order to understand God's heart on each one.

BIBLE STUDY 2
WISDOM AND AUTHORITY

What we transfer to those who come behind us is critical. Whether it is tangible, physical goods, or life lessons—a greater focus on what we pass on to others will help in raising up more kingdom men who impact culture. One of the most dynamic male relationships in Scripture gives us insight into the nature of this transfer. It took place between Moses and Joshua. When we study their relationship, we see that Moses transferred many things to Joshua like insight on how to lead, experience in battle, as well as countless lessons on communicating with God. But one of the more important aspects transferred to Joshua from Moses was the "spirit of wisdom."

Keep in mind, the Bible does not say that Moses passed down wisdom to Joshua. It says he passed down the "spirit of wisdom," specifically by laying his hands on him. Let's take a look at the passage and then examine it through a few questions.

Read Deuteronomy 34:9.

> *Now Joshua the son of Nun was filled with the spirit of wisdom,*
> *for Moses had laid his hands on him; and the sons of Israel listened*
> *to him and did as the LORD had commanded Moses.*
> Deuteronomy 34:9

What was Moses laying his hands on Joshua meant to communicate?

What was the result of Joshua receiving the "spirit of wisdom?"

What are some ways we can model this kind of wisdom transfer today?

Do you think it's even necessary to model it? Why or why not?

In the passage we just looked at, we see how Moses transferred the values and per-spective of the kingdom of God through transferring the "spirit of wisdom" to Joshua. A transfer of kingdom values and perspective can be passed down in many ways and should be passed down to all, but when a person has matured to the point of leading others, it is also important to pass down other things with it as well such as spiritual authority. We first see Moses laying his hands on Joshua back in Numbers 27:23. Then it was to impart spiritual authority.

> *Then he laid his hands on him and commissioned him,*
> *just as the LORD had spoken through Moses.*
> **Numbers 27:23**

How do you know when the time is right to pass on spiritual wisdom and authority to someone you are discipling?

Moses wasn't quick to pass on this spiritual authority to Joshua. He knew that he needed to wait until the time was right. One of the worst things to do to a man is give him authority when he is not mature enough yet to handle it. But once you identify someone as having great potential for future leadership, and you see that he has reached the point of spiritual maturity, it is up to you to similarly pass on spiritual authority.

The transfer of spiritual authority comes when you recognize someone is ready to lead and transfer their spiritual fruit to others. Because Joshua had been a faithful servant, he now received his turn to lead. Joshua, like Moses, would now represent the Lord to the people of Israel. Through his relationship with Moses and his pursuit of the Lord, he gained the wisdom and authority necessary to lead well.

Explain the difference between passing on spiritual wisdom and passing on spiritual authority.

What are some key identifiers you would want to see in a man before commissioning him to further the future by leading others.

Have you ever experienced someone (or yourself) being given spiritual authority too soon? If so, what was the result?

Unfortunately, too many men want to lead without serving first. They want the authority without surrendering. That's backwards. They want to jump out to the front without learning the fundamentals. I believe that's one reason we are witnessing a large number of Christian leaders retire early or become disqualified from the ministry over scandals or misuse of the power given to them. I believe many had been vested with leadership due to the quick rise of digital platforms without first learning to serve.

Joshua had matured to the point where the blessing of spiritual authority was now his. And because he had spent so much time under the tutelage of Moses, he was able to keep the same vision going, albeit in a different style. He had his own methods, but the core of the ministry remained the same.

> *All Israel with their elders and officers and their judges were standing on both sides of the ark before the Levitical priests who carried the ark of the covenant of the LORD, the stranger as well as the native. Half of them stood in front of Mount Gerizim and half of them in front of Mount Ebal, just as Moses the servant of the LORD had given command at first to bless the people of Israel. Then afterward he read all the words of the law, the blessing and the curse, according to all that is written in the book of the law. There was not a word of all that Moses had commanded which Joshua did not read before all the assembly of Israel with the women and the little ones and the strangers who were living among them.*
> **Joshua 8:33-35**

How did Joshua's ministry model Moses' ministry?

Based on our study of Joshua, what are the critical elements to transfer when discipling someone, and what are not as critical to transfer?

Do you need to be discipled yourself? Do you feel like you need to be trained in wisdom and spiritual authority? If so, who might disciple you? Have you considered asking them?

If you feel you are ready, to whom are you seeking to impart wisdom and authority?

Pray about ways God would have you transfer either spiritual wisdom or spiritual authority to someone else. Ask God to help you identify someone you can disciple on a greater level. If no one comes to mind, ask Him to reveal any areas you may still need to grow and develop before discipling others, then seek to pursue that spiritual growth yourself.

So then we pursue the things
which make for peace and the
building up of one another.

ROMANS 14:19

IDENTIFYING KEY INFLUENCERS

START

Last session, you were asked about how to implement small steps of discipleship into your daily rhythms. Let's talk about this for a minute.

As you considered ways to expand your spiritual influence, what incremental steps did you take?

During last session's personal studies, you were challenged to begin identifying where to spend your influence to build the kingdom. This session, we will look more intently at how to identify key influencers.

What would happen to someone who consistently made unwise decisions?

Decisions matter. Choices matter. God has given each of us the opportunity to live with what is known as "free will." Free will simply means that have the ability to choose between potential courses of action without obstruction, yet inherent in each choice is an outcome.

For example, if you choose to walk down the middle of a busy road, you may get hit by a car. However, what we forget to teach others through discipleship is the importance of personal responsibility. Bad outcomes come through bad choices, and choices are made as we exercise free will.

Rising up as a kingdom man means making the connection between our choices and outcomes and showing others the importance of this critical truth. Understanding this principle is essential in identifying potential influencers of the future.

Ask someone to pray before watching the video teaching.

Identifying Key Influencers
WATCH

Use this space to take notes during the video teaching.

MAN UP

Use the following questions to discuss the video teaching.

How do our choices demonstrate that we are serious about influencing others?

On the other hand, how does making poor choices limit our influence?

Have you ever noticed that when one player on a sports team starts playing at a higher level, others rise with him? His standard of expertise and commitment rubs off on those around him and, as a result, the rest of the team has the opportunity to play better as well. Life as a kingdom man rising takes the same posture.

To be a kingdom man is to be an influencer. Life is no longer about yourself, but how you can bring along others also. For a kingdom man to leave a spiritual heritage, he has to identify key influencers.

Read Romans 14:19 together and answer the following questions.

So then we pursue the things which make for peace
and the building up of one another.
Romans 14:19

What does it look like for men to "build up one another?"

Why is pursuing peace an important part of strengthening others in their walk with the Lord?

How does being contentious hinder our influence with others?

Sometimes we can confuse the bravado men seek to exude with actual strength. But bravado in and of itself often lacks true strength. Anytime contention, bravado, or selfishness show up as a dominant force in our lives, division is the natural result.

In order to be an influencer who impacts others for good, a kingdom man must first control his own character and align it under God's rule of love. Feeding a man's need to be on top or have his ego puffed up is one of Satan's number one strategies for limiting the potential positive impact of influence that man can have in the lives of others.

Besides leading us to be contentious, what are some ways men can outmaneuver Satan in his attempts to keep men from rising as kingdom influencers?

How do accountability relationships and authentic conversations serve to keep men grounded in humility and truth?

Are you willing to have those difficult conversations with other men, or allow them to have them with you when things have gotten off track? Why are these essential? Why are these conversations not opposed to being peaceful?

Kingdom men are serious about extending their influence. Influence comes through a number of ways. It could be modeling. It could be through honest conversations. It might be through being willing to admit mistakes and correct them. Whatever the approach, keep in mind that influencing others for good involves making right choices yourself, as well as living with a spirit of biblical love. A leader not only tells the way, but he also shows the way through his own life, words, and behavior.

As this is our last session together, share one or two key truths you've learned through this study you hope to put into practice over the coming months.

What is one way the men in this group can be praying for you as you seek to influence others?

PRAYER.

Father, help us to make right choices so that we can be better positioned to influence others for Your glory and the advancement of Your kingdom. Show us what we need to do in order to help others understand Your will for their lives and rise to become influencers themselves. In Christ's name, amen.

THREE QUALITIES OF A KINGDOM INFLUENCER

Many qualities make up a man of influence, but there are three key traits that can help you either spot a future influencer, or help develop one by focusing on these areas. These are character, competence, and commitment. When a man is solid in all three of these areas, he will lead well by example and influence those around him.

1
A MAN OF CHARACTER

In order to be a kingdom influencer, a man must have personal character. Take a moment to read Acts 6:3 and 1 Timothy 3:8-13. These verses speak to the character qualities of a deacon but, by default, a deacon was to be a man of influence. Thus, these qualities also transfer to kingdom men who seek to influence others. When you are discipling a man to become a key influencer, as he grows, be sure to examine the importance of having a solid character.

A MAN OF COMPETENCE

You may have heard it said that volunteers often have more heart than skill. They might mean well but wind up causing issues in whatever it is they are volunteering at due to a lack of competence in the role. Raising up a kingdom influencer isn't only about sharpening a man's character, but it is also about identifying ways he can develop a greater competence in all that he does. Psalm 78:72 gives us an example of both where it says of David:

So he shepherded them according to the integrity of his heart,
And guided them with his skillful hands.
Psalm 78:72

A MAN OF COMMITMENT

Character and competence are only as good as the commitment behind them. If an NFL team were to draft a highly skilled player, only to have that player quit after a few weeks, they would be worse off than when they first grabbed him. Commitment is that quality which ensures that character and competence have the atmosphere to do their work. Commitment is lacking in our culture today—whether it is to a work role, family, church home, or small group, this lack of commitment negatively impacts everyone in its path. A kingdom influencer must merge character with competence and commitment if he is truly going to leave a lasting impact during his time on earth.

Which of these three qualities do you need to cultivate most in your life?

What are some steps you'll take to cultivate this over the next month?

INFLUENCING INFLUENCERS

You can measure the destiny of a team—whether that be a family, work group, business, church, community, or even a nation—by its leadership. Unfortunately, today we face a crisis of leadership. People don't know who to follow anymore because this crisis has produced a plethora of poor models and mentors and an utter lack of great leaders.

Yet, God's kingdom program is designed around the process of transferring spiritual wisdom, known as discipleship, in order to produce future leaders. One of the primary roles of kingdom men is to lead others in the way they should go. The issue at hand is never whether or not a man is a leader. As a kingdom man, you are a leader by nature of your creation and calling. The issue is whether or not you will be a great leader or a poor one.

Read the following passages and write down how each passage describes biblically-based kingdom leadership.

Titus 1:7-9

1 Timothy 4:12

Hebrews 13:7

Matthew 10:42-45

Galatians 6:9

John 13:34-35

Steadfastness, kindness, love, faith, self-control, dignity, teachability, hospitality and a love for God's Word are some qualities that contribute to making a man a great leader. These are the same qualities men can use to identify future key influencers as well as to help them cultivate these traits at a greater level.

What are some cultural and secular traits that men often look for in identifying future influencers?

In what ways do these differ from the biblical traits listed in the verses above?

How do, or can, these differences contribute to a lack of solid male leadership in our society today?

One of the biggest mistakes we make in raising up future leaders is the assumption that great leadership is taught, not caught. Raising up a generation of key influencers is never to be done in a top-down way. It happens organically and authentically when men share their lives, experiences, and conversations.

Developing key influencers who can solidly speak on biblical truths and navigate the storms of society requires guidance, practice, learning, listening, and so forth. Just like any marriage is dependent on two people contributing for it be great, identifying and raising up a kingdom influencer requires both men to put forth the effort to learn, grow, listen, teach, discern, practice, model, and more.

What would need to change in your life to make room for more relationships with men in which you can grow as well as help others to grow too?

On a scale of 1-10, how important is it to you to increase this level of engagement?

1   10

Not Important   **Very Important**

Great leadership knows how to spot great leadership, and then turn it loose within the boundaries of their own guidance. Coaching trees in the NFL are a great example of this principle at work. The best coaches have multiple assistant coaches who go on to coach teams themselves. You can judge a coach, at least in part, by their coaching tree. In the spiritual realm, kingdom men carry the same capacity to influence others and raise up men who will make a difference in the culture for Christ.

What are some critical elements that make a coaching tree successful at developing future great coaches?

How can we as kingdom men apply some of these elements to our relationships and systems so that we can have a greater collective impact on our society?

Let's be clear. You are not here just for you. You are here for others. You have been crafted and created by God as an instrument of influence for the furthering of His kingdom agenda on earth. Satan has done a great job of getting men to focus on the areas of life which do not lead to generational transfer of kingdom values. But it is time that we rise up as men to take our stand against the enemy's schemes. Paul gives us wisdom for how to accomplish this purpose in 2 Corinthians.

> *For though we walk in the flesh, we do not war according to the flesh, for the weapons of our warfare are not of the flesh, but divinely powerful for the destruction of fortresses. We are destroying speculations and every lofty thing raised up against the knowledge of God, and we are taking every thought captive to the obedience of Christ.*
> **2 Corinthians 10:3-5**

How can we as men do a better job at collectively "destroying speculations and every lofty thing raised up against the knowledge of God"?

Have you ever blindly trusted a friend only to later discover he led you down the wrong path? Describe the role of discernment when it comes to identifying and maintaining accountability and growth-based relationships.

Where do you think our culture could wind up if an army of kingdom men were to rise up for righteousness, justice and the furtherance of God's Word?

Satan tries to get us to forget that we do not wage the battle for influence and leadership in our culture with worldly weapons. We wage this battle through the power of the Spirit and by using weapons of spiritual warfare. One of the primary weapons is the wisdom needed to discern truth from Satan's lies. As we do that, we will see how important it is to help others to do the same. Satan uses deception as a primary tool in keeping men held back from living as the leaders they have been designed to be.

Pray about ways you can both better discern God's role and leading in your life and how you need to grow, as well as how you can live with greater kingdom influence on those around you. As God brings ideas to your mind, ask Him to open the doors and show you the way on how to pursue them. Let Him know you are willing to be used by Him to positively impact the lives He brings within your spheres of influence.

BIBLE STUDY 2
KINGDOM DECLARATION

As we come to the close of our time together studying spiritual concepts of biblical manhood, I wanted to encourage everyone to consider taking part in the Kingdom Declaration located at the back of the book, *Kingdom Men Rising*. Stating your declaration publicly will go far in helping you to carry out the principles you've learned in this study. For your reference, it is being placed in this study as well.

KINGDOM DECLARATION

1. Whereas God created the man to be primarily responsible for advancing His kingdom agenda.
2. Whereas God has positioned men as head of their families.
3. Whereas God holds men accountable and responsible for maintaining an intimate relationship with Him.
4. Whereas God requires men to love and lead their wives.
5. Whereas God has given men the primary responsibility for raising their children.
6. Whereas God has determined for men to oversee the spiritual leadership and direction of the church.
7. Whereas God holds men accountable for the spiritual condition of the culture.
8. Whereas God will hold men accountable at the judgment seat of Christ for how they fulfilled their divinely assigned role and responsibility.

I, _____, declare today that I commit the remainder of my life to fulfill my created calling to function as a kingdom disciple in my walk with God, leadership of my family, commitment to my church, and influencing of my community.

_____
SIGNATURE

_____
DATE

Take a moment to read through this declaration and write down your thoughts on where you need to improve and focus on the most.

What are some ways you can regularly remind yourself of the responsibilities of a kingdom man outlined in the Kingdom Declaration?

Without a doubt, we face a culture that wants to trick us, trip us up, and get us to make the wrong decisions in this life. But the answer to whether we will experience spiritual victory in our walk as men is in our own hands. Our future as families, churches, communities and even as a nation is in our own hands. Satan only appears to be winning this war on the world because kingdom men have not declared to rise up and resist him. It's not because Satan is more powerful. Satan is not more powerful than Christ.

If we, as kingdom men, collectively choose to follow Christ by cultivating a relationship with Him and submitting to His rule, we will defeat the enemy at every turn. Any other path we pursue will result in further destruction. The choice is ours to make. The time to make that choice is now.

It is high time we rise up as one voice and one example for each other, our families, our churches, our communities, and our land. It's time we take our positions on the field. Grab what you've got. Use it. Make your moves. Lead with love. Disciple those within your spheres of influence. Invest in your own spiritual growth and maturity.

Sure, the opposition we face in our world today as men is rearing its ugly head on every level. But you and I both know the One who knows how this story ends. We know the One who knows the end from the beginning. The One who crafted and created you has already determined that His purposes WILL be carried out.

How is living as a kingdom man influencing other men entirely dependent upon God's strength and work in our lives?

Read Isaiah 46:10 and answer the following questions:

*Declaring the end from the beginning, and from ancient times
things which have not been done, saying, 'My purpose will be
established, and I will accomplish all My good pleasure."*
Isaiah 46:10

**What are some things and outcomes which you believe would qualify as God's
"good pleasure?"**

**In what ways can you participate more fully in pursuing the carrying out and
accomplishing all of God's "good pleasure?"**

Describe what you feel knowing that God's purposes will be established.

Take time to examine your life and choices based on what you have learned in this study.
Identify where you are making the greatest impact and look for how you can improve
your influence over others for God and for good. Then, take a moment to write out your
own prayer to conclude this time of study together. Focus on what you are grateful for
and what you would like to see improved in your own life, and in the lives of those you
love—through your influence.

Dear God, _____

KINGDOM MEN RISING

TONY EVANS

D-GROUP GUIDE

If you're reading this, you likely care about discipleship. You desire to be a kingdom man living under God's kingdom agenda. Being in a small group or a Sunday School class is one means believers use to go deeper in the Christian life. However, increasingly, people want closer and more tight-knit community. To this end we've provided a guide to facilitate those kinds of small groups.

WHAT IS A D-GROUP? As opposed to an open small group or a Sunday School class (meaning everyone is welcome), a D-Group is a closed group that three or four people join by invitation and commitment.

WHAT'S THE PURPOSE OF A D-GROUP? These groups are for Christians who desire to walk more closely with the Lord. The smaller nature of the group allows a more concentrated level of accountability and opens up discussions that are more personal than in a standard group meeting.

WHY DO I NEED A D-GROUP? We're not meant to live the Christian life alone. You'll need support as you seek to live as a kingdom man. Opening yourself up to people in a smaller environment encourages participation from you and from those who may not feel comfortable opening up in a larger group.

Additionally, D-Groups give others permission to speak into your life for encouragement, accountability, and prayer.

WHAT'S REQUIRED OF ME? The goal of these groups is deeper discipleship and accountability. Achieving this goal requires commitment. Plan to meet for one hour. Be willing to attend and participate each week. Be willing to be open and honest about your spiritual condition and about ways you're struggling. Be willing to hold what's said in the group in confidence. What's said should remain in the group as a means of building trust with one another. Finally, be willing to pray and support one another. Allow the relationships to extend beyond the group meeting itself.

HOW TO USE THESE GUIDES

A D-Group guide is provided for each week of this study. These guides are meant to be used in addition to the weekly group session but can be also used by people who aren't meeting with a group. However, these guides work best if participants have seen the week's video teaching by Dr. Evans. Each D-Group guide is two pages and includes the following elements.

SUMMARY. Summary of key ideas from the session.

D-GROUP QUESTIONS. In addition to the article, a passage of Scripture with some commentary and three questions are provided. These open-ended questions are designed to encourage men to open up about their struggles and successes for the purposes of growth and accountability.

SESSION 1
CHOSEN FOR THE CHALLENGE

SUMMARY

As a kingdom man, God has given you a purpose to live out, a divine design to fulfill. This session speaks to your unique calling to provide the foundational framework upon which your influence can rest and rise.

KEY QUESTIONS

Do you feel chosen by God for the challenge of being a kingdom man? Why or why not?

What are some ways we can embrace the calling to be a kingdom man every day?

How can intentional friendships, cultivated in groups like this keep us accountable and on track to stay focused on the challenge ahead?

Share some expectations you have for the other men in the group.

SESSION 2
DRY BONES DANCING

SUMMARY

Some men are held back because they are unable or unwilling to overcome Satan's distractions and trust in God's plans, purposes, and promises. However God can take a stale or declining spiritual life and give it renewed vitality.

KEY QUESTIONS

Share which of Satan's distractions you are most prone to follow.

What are a couple of ways other kingdom men can hold you accountable and help you refocus on God?

Describe your current proximity to God. How is He giving you spiritual vitality?

What is a promise of God you are focusing on this week? Explain.

SESSION 3
GET UP

SUMMARY

Sometimes life's difficulties knock us out, beat us down, or get us off the field completely. Standing up after you've been knocked down is rarely a solo experience. It takes others to come alongside you to lift you, encourage you, and strengthen you until you can once again stand on your own.

KEY QUESTIONS

Who has been a key encourager to you in your spiritual life? How can you be similarly encouraging to others?

Where do you need to "get up" and overcome spiritual lameness?

Review the steps on pages 48-49. Which one is most helpful to you right now? Where could you stand to grow?

Is there a man you know who needs to "get up" and take hold of his spiritual health? How can you help him?

SESSION 4
GET GOING

SUMMARY

Too many men today have identified with too many false gods. Men need to step up, get going, and move away from the lifeless idols robbing them of spiritual vitality and impact. When we put away our idols and embrace God's better plan for our lives, He will use us to do something bigger than what we could have ever done on our own.

KEY QUESTIONS

What are the most common idols that plague men today? Where do you see these in your friendships or in the culture around you?

When might men need help moving away from idols? Why should we help other men see this need?

Recall the story of Gideon from this week's study in Judges 6. How did God alter Gideon's identity? Where does God need to shape your identity?

How do healthy spiritual habits break us from idols? What habits do you need to cultivate?

SESSION 5
GET ALONG

SUMMARY

Much of the chaos and defeat we are experiencing today is a result of illegitimate division in the church. The division in our culture, and in our church, racially, politically, and socially needs a group of kingdom men who will rise to dispel it while insisting on unity through all we say and do.

KEY QUESTIONS

Why do you think demonstrating "love for one another" reveals to onlookers that we are Christ's kingdom disciples?

How can we be men who contribute to harmony and peace instead of division?

Is there any area of your life where you are pursuing division instead of unity? What changes do you need to make?

What does it look like to be a kingdom man who preserves kingdom unity?

SESSION 6
SETTING THE STAGE

SUMMARY

Far too often, God is waiting on us as men to do something before He will make His move. Whether it is Moses holding out the rod before He parts the sea, or Peter keeping his eyes on Jesus before He rescues him from the storm—God frequently waits to see how we respond in faith before He fully reveals His hand in our lives.

KEY QUESTIONS

Where might you need to embrace God's faithfulness and follow Him?

Why is it so easy for us to get overwhelmed in "flood" seasons? What steps can we take to depend on God and keep our heads above water?

Where do you need to listen to, stand, and obey God?

Why is it better to trust in God's power than in human limitations?

SESSION 7
FURTHERING THE FUTURE

SUMMARY

Part of being a kingdom man is the successfully passing on kingdom values. The buck doesn't stop with you. We desperately need more men to realize this and rise up to fulfill this great purpose in the body of Christ today. We further the future by passing the gift of discipleship.

KEY QUESTIONS

Read Proverbs 13:22. What does this look like in your life? How might a man with no physical descendants impact the next generation?

To pass on kingdom values we have to be generationally minded and not merely personally fulfilled." Describe the differences between being "generationally minded" as opposed to "personally fulfilled." Which are you? Explain.

Discuss ways that each of you in the d-group can add small, yet intentional, steps of discipleship to your normal routine.

What are you passing on to the next generation?

SESSION 8
IDENTIFYING KEY INFLUENCERS

SUMMARY

Rising up as a kingdom man means making the connection between our choices and outcomes and showing others the importance of this critical truth. Understanding this principle is essential in identifying potential influencers of the future. For kingdom men to rise, the need to be identified and trained.

KEY QUESTIONS

How can you begin to build up kingdom influencers within your spheres of influence?

What does it look like for men to "build up one another?" Why is pursuing peace an important part of strengthening others in their walk with the Lord?

What would happen if each man in this group decided to identify and invest in a key influence for the sake of the kingdom?

What is your most important takeaway from this study? Who will you share it with?

NOTES

APPENDIX
THE URBAN ALTERNATIVE

The Urban Alternative (TUA) equips, empowers and unites Christians to impact individuals, families, churches and communities through a thoroughly kingdom agenda worldview. In teaching truth, we seek to transform lives.

The core cause of the problems we face in our personal lives, homes, churches and societies is a spiritual one; therefore, the only way to address it is spiritually. We've tried a political, social, economic and even a religious agenda.

IT'S TIME FOR A KINGDOM AGENDA.

The kingdom agenda can be defined as the visible manifestation of the comprehensive rule of God over every area of life.

The unifying central theme throughout the Bible is the glory of God and the advancement of His kingdom. The conjoining thread from Genesis to Revelation—from beginning to end—is focused on one thing: God's glory through advancing God's kingdom.

When you do not recognize that theme, the Bible becomes disconnected stories that are great for inspiration but seem to be unrelated in purpose and direction. Understanding the role of the kingdom in Scripture increases the relevancy of this several thousand-year-old text to your day-to-day living, because the kingdom is not only then; it is now.

The absence of the kingdom's influence in our personal lives, family lives, churches, and communities has led to a deterioration in our world of immense proportions:

- People live segmented, compartmentalized lives because they lack God's kingdom worldview.
- Families disintegrate because they exist for their own satisfaction rather than for the kingdom.
- Churches are limited in the scope of their impact because they fail to comprehend that the goal of the church is not the church itself, but the kingdom.
- Communities have nowhere to turn to find real solutions for real people who have real problems because the church has become divided, in-grown and unable to transform the cultural and political landscape in any relevant way.

The kingdom agenda offers us a way to see and live life with a solid hope by optimizing the solutions of heaven. When God is no longer the final and authoritative standard under which all else falls, order and hope leaves with Him. But the reverse of that is true as well: as long as you have God, you have hope. If God is still in the picture, and as long as His agenda is still on the table, it's not over.

Even if relationships collapse, God will sustain you. Even if finances dwindle, God will keep you. Even if dreams die, God will revive you. As long as God and His rule are still the overarching standard in your life, family, church and community, there is always hope.

OUR WORLD NEEDS THE KING'S AGENDA.
OUR CHURCHES NEED THE KING'S AGENDA.
OUR FAMILIES NEED THE KING'S AGENDA.

We've put together a three-part plan to direct us to heal the divisions and strive for unity as we move toward the goal of truly being one nation under God. This three-part plan calls us to assemble with others in unity, address the issues that divide us, and to act together for social impact. Following this plan, we will see individuals, families, churches and communities transformed as we follow God's kingdom agenda in every area of our lives. You can request this plan by emailing info@tonyevans.org or by going online to tonyevans.org.

In many major cities, there is a loop that drivers can take when they want to get somewhere on the other side of the city but don't necessarily want to head straight through downtown. This loop will take you close enough to the city so that you can see its towering buildings and skyline, but not close enough to actually experience it.

This is precisely what we, as a culture, have done with God. We have put Him on the "loop" of our personal, family, church and community lives. He's close enough to be at hand should we need Him in an emergency, but far enough away that He can't be the center of who we are.

We want God on the "loop," not the King of the Bible who comes downtown into the very heart of our ways. Leaving God on the "loop" brings about dire consequences as we have seen in our own lives and with others. But when we make God, and His rule, the centerpiece of all we think, do or say, it is then that we will experience Him in the way He longs for us to experience Him.

He wants us to be kingdom people with kingdom minds set on fulfilling His kingdom's purposes. He wants us to pray, as Jesus did, "Not my will, but Thy will be done." Because His is the kingdom, the power, and the glory.

There is only one God, and we are not Him. As King and Creator, God calls the shots. It is only when we align ourselves underneath His comprehensive hand that we will access His full power and authority in all spheres of life: personal, familial, ecclesiastical, and government.

As we learn how to govern ourselves under God, we then transform the institutions of family, church, and society using a biblically based kingdom worldview.

Under Him, we touch heaven and change earth.

To achieve our goal, we use a variety of strategies, approaches and resources for reaching and equipping as many people as possible.

BROADCAST MEDIA

Millions of individuals experience The Alternative with Dr. Tony Evans through the daily radio broadcast playing on nearly 1,400 Radio outlets and in over 130 countries. The broadcast can also be seen on several television networks, and is available online at tonyevans.org. You can also listen or view the daily broadcast by downloading the Tony Evans app for free in the App store. Over 30,000,000 message downloads/streams occur each year.

LEADERSHIP TRAINING

The Tony Evans Training Center (TETC) facilitates a comprehensive discipleship platform which provides an educational program that embodies the ministry philosophy of Dr. Tony Evans as expressed through the kingdom agenda. The training courses focus on leadership development and discipleship in the following five tracks:

- Bible & Theology
- Personal Growth
- Family and Relationships
- Church Health and Leadership Development
- Society and Community Impact Strategies

The TETC program includes courses for both local and online students. Furthermore, TETC programming includes course work for non-student attendees. Pastors, Christian leaders and Christian laity, both local and at a distance, can seek out The Kingdom Agenda Certificate for personal, spiritual and professional development. For more information, visit: TonyEvansTraining.org

The Kingdom Agenda Pastors (KAP) provides a viable network for like-minded pastors who embrace the kingdom agenda philosophy. Pastors have the opportunity to go deeper with Dr. Tony Evans as they are given greater biblical knowledge, practical applications and resources to impact individuals, families, churches and communities. KAP welcomes senior and associate pastors of all churches. KAP also offers an annual

Summit held each year in Dallas with intensive seminars, workshops and resources. For more information, visit: KAFellowship.org

Pastors' Wives Ministry, founded by Dr. Lois Evans, provides counsel, encouragement and spiritual resources for pastors' wives as they serve with their husbands in the ministry. A primary focus of the ministry is the KAP Summit that offers senior pastors' wives a safe place to reflect, renew and relax along with training in personal development, spiritual growth and care for their emotional and physical well-being. For more information, visit: LoisEvans.org

KINGDOM COMMUNITY IMPACT

The outreach programs of The Urban Alternative seek to provide positive impact to individuals, churches, families and communities through a variety of ministries. We see these efforts as necessary to our calling as a ministry and essential to the communities we serve. With training on how to initiate and maintain programs to adopt schools, or provide homeless services, or partner toward unity and justice with the local police precincts, which creates a connection between the police and our community, we, as a ministry, live out God's kingdom agenda according to our Kingdom Strategy for Community Transformation.

The Kingdom Strategy for Community Transformation is a three-part plan that equips churches to have a positive impact on their communities for the kingdom of God. It also provides numerous practical suggestions for how this three-part plan can be implemented in your community, and it serves as a blueprint for unifying churches around the common goal of creating a better world for all of us. For more information, visit: TonyEvans.org and click on the link to access the 3-Point Plan.

National Church Adopt-a-School Initiative (NCAASI) prepares churches across the country to impact communities by using public schools as the primary vehicle for effecting positive social change in urban youth and families. Leaders of churches, school districts, faith-based organizations and other nonprofit organizations are equipped with the knowledge and tools to forge partnerships and build strong social service delivery systems. This training is based on the comprehensive church-based community impact strategy conducted by Oak Cliff Bible Fellowship. It addresses such areas as economic development, education, housing, health revitalization, family renewal and racial reconciliation. We assist churches in tailoring the model to meet specific needs of their communities while simultaneously addressing the spiritual and moral frame of reference. Training events are held annually in the Dallas area at Oak Cliff Bible Fellowship. For more information, visit: ChurchAdoptaSchool.org

Athlete's Impact (AI) exists as an outreach both into and through the sports arena. Coaches can be the most influential factor in young people's lives, even ahead of their parents. With the growing rise of fatherlessness in our culture, more young people are looking to their coaches for guidance, character development, practical needs and hope. After coaches on the influencer scale fall athletes. Athletes (whether professional or amateur) influence younger athletes and kids within their spheres of impact. Knowing this, we have made it our aim to equip and train coaches and athletes on how to live out and utilize their God-given roles for the benefit of the kingdom. We aim to do this through our iCoach App as well as resources such as The Playbook: A Life Strategy Guide for Athletes. For more information, visit: ICoachApp.org

Tony Evans Films ushers in positive life change through compelling video-shorts, animation and feature-length films. We seek to build kingdom disciples through the power of story. We use a variety of platforms for viewer consumption and have over 100,000,000+ digital views. We also merge video-shorts and film with relevant Bible study materials to bring people to the saving knowledge of Jesus Christ and to strengthen the body of Christ worldwide. Tony Evans Films released the first feature-length film, Kingdom Men Rising, in April 2019 in over 800 theaters nationwide, in partnership with Lifeway Films. The second release, Journey With Jesus, in partnership with RightNow Media.

RESOURCE DEVELOPMENT

We are fostering lifelong learning partnerships with the people we serve by providing a variety of published materials. Dr. Evans has published more than 125 unique titles based on over 50 years of preaching whether that is in booklet, book or Bible study format. He also holds the honor of writing and publishing the first full-Bible commentary and study Bible by an African American, released in 2019. This Bible sits in permanent display as a historic release, in The Museum of the Bible in Washington, D.C.

For more information, and a complimentary copy of Dr. Evans' devotional newsletter, call (800) 800-3222 or write TUA at P.O. Box 4000, Dallas TX 75208, or visit us online

WWW.TONYEVANS.ORG

TONY EVANS

NO MORE EXCUSES

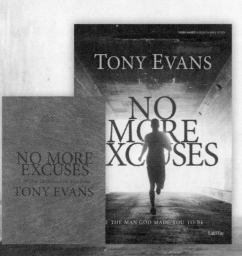

Sometimes circumstances in life make it difficult for men to be all God wants them to be. But Tony Evans urges men to stop looking at their circumstances as excuses and instead to see them as challenges and opportunities for success. Exploring the examples of men of God throughout the Bible, these resources will challenge you to lay down your excuses, stop compromising, and fight to be a man of character and commitment.

ALSO AVAILABLE:
No More Excuses:
A 90-Day Devotional for Men

Lifeway

Building kingdom disciples.

At The Urban Alternative, our heart is to build kingdom disciples—a vision that starts with the individual and expands to the family, the church and the nation. The more than 50-year teaching ministry of Tony Evans has allowed us to reach a world in need with:

The Alternative – Our flagship radio program brings hope and comfort to an audience of millions on over 1,400 radio outlets across the country.

tonyevans.org – Our library of teaching resources provides solid Bible teaching through the inspirational books and sermons of Tony Evans.

Tony Evans Training Center – Experience the adventure of God's Word with our online classroom, providing at-your-own-pace courses for your PC or mobile device. Visit tonyevanstraining.org.

Tony Evans app – This popular resource for finding inspiration on-the-go has had over 20,000,000 launches. It's packed with audio and video clips, devotionals, Scripture readings and dozens of other tools.

tonyevans.org

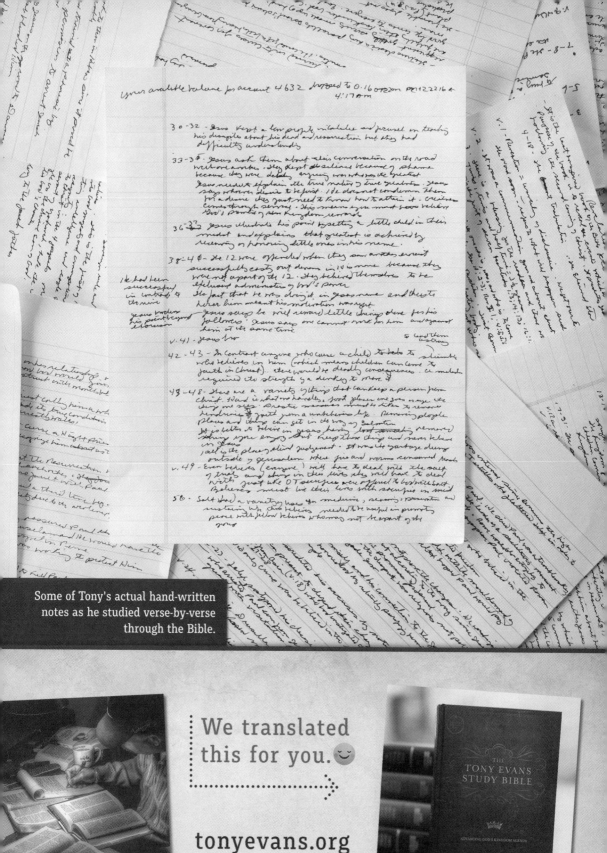

Some of Tony's actual hand-written notes as he studied verse-by-verse through the Bible.

We translated
this for you. 😊

tonyevans.org

THE TONY EVANS STUDY BIBLE

ALSO FROM
DR. TONY EVANS

U-TURNS
Reversing the Consequences
in Your Life

Learn to align your life choices
under God's Word and change the
direction of your life. (6 sessions)

Leader Kit $99.99
Bible Study Book $14.99

PATHWAYS
From Providence to Purpose

Use the biblical account of Esther
to discover your own pathway to
purpose as you learn and apply
principles of God's providence.
(6 sessions)

Leader Kit $99.99
Bible Study Book $14.99

DETOURS
The Unpredictable Path
to Your Destiny

Find hope in understanding that
the sudden or seemingly endless
detours in life are God's way of
moving you from where you are to
where He wants you to be.
(6 sessions)

Leader Kit $99.99
Bible Study Book $14.99

KINGDOM AGENDA
Living Life God's Way

Learn to apply biblical kingdom principles to everyday realities for the individual, the family, the church, or the nation. (6 sessions)

Leader Kit $99.99
Bible Study Book $14.99

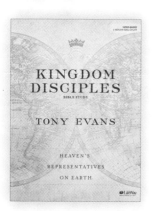

KINGDOM DISCIPLES
Heaven's Representatives on Earth

Develop a confidence and urgency to fulfill your primary responsibility to be a disciple and to make other disciples. (6 sessions)

Leader Kit $99.99
Bible Study Book $14.99

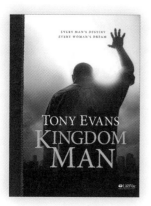

KINGDOM MAN
Every Man's Destiny, Every Woman's Dream

Challenge and equip yourself to fully understand your position under God as well as your position over what God has given you. (6 sessions)

Leader Kit $99.99
Bible Study Book $14.99

Prices and availability subject to change without notice.

Become the man that Jesus is calling you to be.

Through an examination of landmark texts from the Bible and historical biblical figures, this Bible study will exhort you to exercise the God-given place in the home, community, and culture you were created for.

Kingdom Men Rising offers a Bible study experience that will give you a Kingdom understanding, vision, and perspective in crucial areas such as identity and responsibilities. Along the way, Dr. Evans shares practical steps on how to become a man who leads his world well.

This *Bible Study Book* provides biblical content, learning activities, group experiences for eight sessions, and additional study material for smaller discipleship groups.

- See manhood from God's perspective.

- Understand great men of the Bible and imitate their faith.

- Develop a biblical understanding of masculinity.

- Find practical encouragement for becoming a godly man.

- Gain a healthy understanding of God-honoring sexuality.

- Overcome addiction and other emotional setbacks.

- Become an active influence for the Lord in your home.

- Leverage your Kingdom authority to point others to biblical manhood.

ADDITIONAL RESOURCES

KINGDOM MEN RISING LEADER KIT
Includes resources for leading an eight-session group study: one *Bible Study Book*, one DVD with teaching videos from Tony Evans, and a code for access to digital video downloads.

DIGITAL CONTENT
An *eBook* and video teaching sessions are available at lifeway.com/kingdommenrising